RACHEL EFFECT

An Unraveling Revelation of the Real You

LAUREN MCNEELY

ISBN: 979-8-9916058-0-9

This book is a memoir. It reflects the author's present recollections of experiences over time. Some names and characteristics have been changed, some events have been compressed, and some dialogue has been recreated.

I dedicate this book to Rachel and Leah. Thank you for your raw emotions, angry antics, and heart-wrenching prayers to God. Thank you for pleading with Him to become someone Jacob would love and someone who could have children. I'm thankful for your story. Your lives were not lived in vain, and God has used them to bring revelation and a new term to my life: *The Rachel Effect*. Leah, we've all encountered the prettier sister, and Rachel, we've all wanted to do something we couldn't. So, thank you for living real and raw and for showcasing God's glory in ways we can relate to thousands of years later.

Contents

Introduction

My son, do not regard lightly the discipline of the Lord, nor be weary when reproved by him. For the Lord disciplines the one he loves and chastises every son whom he receives.

Hebrews 12:5–6

God is gracious. He reveals to us areas of weakness. He also reveals areas of deception. I have experienced the discipline of the Lord in the most heartbreakingly beautiful way. Hebrews 12:13 says, "…so that what is lame may not be put out of joint but rather be healed."

Again, God is so gracious. In His graciousness, He revealed to me that I have been comparing myself to others and creating an ideal version of myself for most of my life. He didn't leave me there, but rather He revealed to me my motivations and how my belief system was wrong—a belief system that survived the sinner's prayer and waters of baptism.

A belief system that told me I wasn't enough, and by comparing myself to others, I could look around and see what looked better and attempt to become it on my own.

A belief system that guided my motivations to please Him and to take what He had given me in a purpose-filled life even after salvation and do it myself, for myself.

On mission *for* Jesus—not co-missioned *with* Jesus. And I stopped. I said to Jesus, "I don't want to do things for You anymore. I want to do them with You. I don't just want to look at You, but I want to look *with* You. See what You are seeing. Be side by side and face to face all at the same time!"

And then *The Rachel Effect* was revealed to me. I understood it and related to it. I wanted to kill my need for comparison once and for all. And while writing this, I've had to stop my imagination from wandering—wandering into speaking engagements, book tours, and mass publication of this book. I've had to say, "NO." No to my ideal self and yes to Jesus because He is with me always, even to the end of the age. Always. Like when I drift off and plan my acceptance speech for my Pulitzer Prize, and when I'm engaging with His Spirit and typing away in humble obedience. I have said, "Even if no one reads this, I need to write it." I'm half telling the truth. But it's not long before I'm on a stage, in an amazing outfit, looking awesome, and humbly staring in awe at the wow factor of said obedience…in my mind, of course.

The words in this book have been lived in, and will continue to be, as I—and prayerfully you—live out this life with Jesus, all the while becoming like Him!

Chapter One

THE COMPARISON TRAP

If Only I Could Be Like Her

S he was so pretty. Like really pretty—the pretty that boys like. The pretty that makes it in magazines. She was so perfectly trendy too. She always looked good no matter what she had on. Who looks good in sweatpants and a messy bun? She did. She was so thin. Not too thin that it was gross—the kind of thin where nothing was out of place. From-bikini-to-ball-gown thin.

She was a go-getter so whatever she wanted, she got. She was confident. The kind of confidence that fought through insecurity and won. She had the Midas touch; everything she touched turned to gold. She was unapologetic and a tad aloof. And she was disinterested enough to make you beg for her attention.

I wanted to be her, but knew I never could be.

But I was quite the opposite. Fat. Not ugly, but fat enough to distort the beauty underneath. As people would so generously put it, "You'd be so pretty if you lost weight." Ugh, nothing looked good on me. *Could I be invisible, please?* Shopping was painful. I'd pass by the clothes "she" would wear and think *someday* while on my way to the men's big and tall section to buy the biggest T-shirt I could find.

My efforts were never enough. Now don't get me wrong; I would hear the roar of applause and feel a sense of success but only in my mind before the painstaking silence of reality when I tried something new to no avail. Everything I touched fell apart. I was a people pleaser.

Oh, can I just do one more thing for you to like me? Please?

How could I bridge the gap of who I was and who I wanted to be?

Who was she? "She" was someone I had compared myself to for years. It wasn't one person. My "her" was a compilation of comparison—a created ideal image I had added and subtracted to over the years as I looked around and saw what I wanted in other people but didn't have myself. It's true. I wanted to be someone who didn't actually exist, but she was real to me.

I believed I wasn't enough just as I was. I believed I could never, and would never, be her. The image of her was so emblazoned on my mind that every step I took toward being her paled in comparison, which reinforced what I knew to be true:

I will never be her.

She was better. Why? Simply because her life looked perfect. Or at least I thought it was. So, without knowing, she subconsciously became the standard for the perfect life. *My* perfect life, lived by *my* ideal self. She had it all, according to what I believed was *all*. She was who I wanted to be—someone I was never meant to be, but I didn't know that yet. In my ignorance, I punished myself every time I didn't reach the pinnacle of her in my mind. Even more than that, I undermined every effort and attempt at success because it bucked up against the true reality that I will never be her so I don't deserve success.

10

No matter how thin, successful, or cool I become, it will never happen.

I did this over and over again. I tried and tried with all my heart, or should I say half my heart? One half mocked the optimist that kept on trying. The other half would undo my progress in order to prove itself to be true. Nevertheless, I kept trying and kept trying, and then tried once again. Trying became an anesthetic to the pain of never becoming and staying in the cycle of *maybe, someday, if just this once, if only, I could be.*

A great distraction exists in the attempt to become: I would never actually have to become. I know that doesn't make sense, but it kind of does. By always trying to attain *the* perfection—or the perceived perfection—of her, I would never have to actually become her. I could lull myself into a delusional complacency and continue trying to be the her I had created in my mind. Never achieving it—No, of course not. And that would be okay because I was keeping myself busy.

I'm busy trying. Busy feeling productive and heading toward a goal that could never be reached. At least I can say I'm goal oriented, right?

And as I try—as I drift farther and farther away from who I was created to be—I lose any sense of who I am, of who I am supposed to be.

Because after all, I'm supposed to be her.

Why Is She Better Than Me?

There is something wrong with me. I haven't quite been able to put my finger on it. It's just an innate knowing deep inside. I don't seem to fit into the world around me. I suppose you could call me the black sheep of my family. My friends and family don't seem to get me.

I'm not sure if I even get myself. I'm not enough because I'm not her, and she is the standard, she is the goal. If I achieve that goal, well then I'll be enough.

How did I come to this conclusion? Why did I come to this conclusion? Why the assumption that she is better than me, that her life is better than mine, and I should do everything in my power to become like her?

Simple. I believed it.

Proverbs 23:7 (NKJV) says, "For as he thinks in his heart, so is he." I thought it way down deep in my heart:

I'm not enough.

As I compared myself to others, thoughts came, and from those thoughts a belief system was formed. This belief system said that what I had and who I was wasn't good enough. The seemingly innocent art of comparison left me longing for a life I believed I should have but did not have. I worked hard creating this belief system. I used my imagination to reinforce it, dreaming of what I should look like, what I should have, and what I should be doing with my life.

What's Your Selfie Self?

Close your eyes. Well, you can't while you're reading! But take a minute and imagine your perfect self—your selfie self. The self you would give a standing ovation for. You at your very best. Did you do it? Wasn't it great?

I'll share my selfie self with you. I wake up in the morning. I live in a fabulous house on the beach. I put on my Lululemon jogging outfit and head outside for a quick three-to-four-mile run on the beach. Afterward, I come in. Sweating—not dripping—it's more like

Hollywood glistening. I make a breakfast protein smoothie. Of course, when I drink it, I'm in slow motion. I then run upstairs and see my incredibly handsome husband getting our baby up and ready for the day. After giving him a quick kiss, I take a shower in my amazing, state-of-the-art bathroom overlooking the ocean. I walk into my closest and walk out dressed, looking incredible. I hug my baby for a photo-op moment and then jump on a quick conference call. I make lots of decisions and give lots of directions—friendly, kind, but assertive and straightforward. I'm the owner of a very profitable yet well-meaning company. All we do is help, support, and care for people. Yet it's still a very successful company. I am very successful. I have breakfast with my husband and baby. Shortly after, friends unexpectedly pop in for a visit, but that's okay because I'm flexible and my house looks perfect. I enjoy my time with them before having to quickly resolve a work crisis. Afterward, I head off to a photo shoot for my book cover while I laugh with my assistant and sip a latte. And so on and so on.

What does your selfie-self look like? How does it differ from the person you are today?

Doesn't this sound impressive? Of course, it changes slightly from time to time. But ultimately, it's the image I've created to visually project myself into the life of "her." Harmless, right?

The Comparison Trap has Been Around for a While

I am not alone in this. I read about a particular girl a while ago and was shocked to find out she had a "her" too. When I first read about this girl, I had a pretty harsh reaction toward what I learned about her. My thoughts went from *He's just not that into you* to *Get a grip* and *Face it, you're the ugly one.* Yes, I know that's harsh.

Her name was Leah. She had weak eyes. She had a sister whose name was Rachel; she was the beautiful one. These are a couple of women in the Bible who had a pretty rough road ahead of them.

Here's the quick backstory. Jacob was a twin and the son of Issac. Issac was the promised child to Abraham, so he was a pretty special boy. Isaac marries Jacob's mother, Rebekah, in a fabulous fix-up that's worth reading about in Genesis 24. Sometime after, Rebekah has twins, Esau and Jacob. Esau was Daddy's favorite and Jacob was a momma's boy. Esau was in line for the blessing—the money, the status, the rights to the family riches, and most of all, the promise of God to fulfill His covenant through Abraham. Since Jacob was Rebekah's favorite, she worked out a plan for him to steal the blessing. And it worked. Jacob got the blessing, but he also got the wrath of his brother. So, he fled to his uncle Laban's house, where he met Rachel (who was technically his cousin, but we won't go there right now). Oh, how Jacob loved Rachel. In fact, it was love at first sight. She was beautiful in his eyes, and the Bible tells us that she really was lovely. In the English Standard Version, it says, "Leah's eyes were weak, but Rachel was beautiful in form and appearance" (Genesis 29:17).

Let's stop right there for a minute. Come on...we can say Rachel was beautiful, but do we have to know that Leah had weak eyes? What does the Bible mean by *weak eyes*? There is a lot of speculation about what the writer of Genesis was implying with the inclusion of that description of Leah. Was it just a nice way to say she was ugly? Even plain and flat-out unattractive? I thought God didn't make ugly, does He? I know that what He makes is good. So, can ugly be good? Let's suffice it to say that Rachel was described as beautiful in form and appearance, and Leah wasn't. Whether it was physical or an inner oomph that seems to attract men, we can assume by its inclusion that it's important for us to know how they were different even if it seems unfair to Leah. Poor Leah.

Anyway, Jacob said he would work for his uncle Laban for seven years in order to marry Rachel, and Laban agreed.

There's more to the story. It gets pretty juicy, but before we go on, let's talk about Leah and Rachel's relationship for a minute.

Rachel was the younger sister, and she was the one at the well when Jacob entered the town. She was a shepherdess getting the animals water when she first met Jacob. She was a working woman. She took care of things and got things done. Where was Leah? Was she tending to things at home? We don't know. It wasn't important enough to mention.

Disclaimer: I believe that every word in the Bible is true. It is a redemptive story of how God has reconciled us back to Himself through the death, burial, and resurrection of his Son, Jesus. So, I know every word recorded is true and relevant to that truth and that truth alone. However, for the purpose of this book, I'm going to speculate a bit. Not only *can* we dissect these stories, but we should. These were people just like you and me, so their feelings and emotions, their hurts, pains, and successes are relatable to us, even now.

We don't know what we don't know, but we do know Rachel was prettier. Rachel had responsibilities in her father's business. I have to assume that in Leah's weak eyes, Rachel was better than her, and Rachel was Leah's "her."

Ugh. Another comparison trap.

Leah had to have compared herself to her younger, more beautiful and successful sister. You know how I know? Because she was human! And as you continue to get to know these girls, you'll see that the text supports this theory through prayers of anguish, competition, and some crazy drama.

We constantly compare ourselves to others. As women, we look at other women. We look them up and down to take a quick inventory of their size, shape, hair, makeup, outfit, etc. Most of the time, unconsciously. It's not to judge them—well, sometimes it is. Many times, we celebrate their good fortune. However, we often compare them to the standard of ourselves. If they look (either physically or positionally) better in any way, we will disqualify ourselves yet again—not consciously, but we do it.

I sometimes call it body-part shopping.

What does this look like in real life or at least in my life? It's crazy—my mind can create an ideal me during an innocent walk in the park. As I stroll through the winding path and see the blue sky, green grass, and people running, jumping, and enjoying this moment in time, I think about how I like that girl's legs because they're so long and thin and how this girl's eyes are such a unique shade of green. I even think about another one's feet. Yes, even feet.

It's sneaky. I may not be thinking, *Hmmm, how can I rip myself apart and minimize the significance of others in one fell swoop?* No, I say to myself, *I'm admiring the beauty all around me,* while secretly putting myself down for not measuring up.

Or, if you're less shallow than me, you can do it in your place of business or at school. You can dissect the intellect and performance of those around you—by the words they use, the way your boss responds positively to them, and how quickly they've climbed the corporate ladder. You can put all of that together in one big, combined assumption and make yourself feel pretty inadequate rather quickly.

If we do that with strangers, how much more do we compare ourselves with those close to us?

Where does this come from? If we believed that we were good enough, special enough, important enough, or pretty enough, would we still compare ourselves to others?

What is comparison anyway? Where does it come from?

First, we'll define it. "Comparison" is a noun that means "a consideration or estimate of the similarities or dissimilarities between two things or people."[i]

Notice that it's defined as a consideration or estimate of. A consideration is "careful thought, usually over a period of time, and an estimate is a judgment of the worth or character of someone or something."[ii]

I'll put it in my own words. Comparison is careful thought, possibly over a period of time, that puts a value or worth on the similarities or differences between two people or things.

If I were comparing ice cream and spaghetti, I would quickly determine they are similar in that they're both foods, but they're dissimilar because one is sweet and the other is not. And the only reason I'd be comparing them in the first place is to come to a conclusion about one or the other. So, I'd want to think carefully in order to put a value or worth on their similarities and differences to come to the conclusion I'm seeking.

Let's say I want to compare ice cream and spaghetti and their effects on blood sugar levels in the body. I would see that they're different because ice cream has added sugar and spaghetti turns into sugar once digested, but they both increase blood sugar levels.

Harmless, right? This doesn't make one better than the other. It just is.

So, why *is* comparison harmful? It's merely a tool. Why do we use it to gauge our appropriate place in this world? Why do we allow it to stifle our voice or minimize our purpose? Why does it have the power to stop us in our tracks? Why does it either validate us or disqualify us? Why do we use comparison to motivate us either positively or negatively?

Can our inward desires (selfie self) combined with society's point of view (approval) of us drive us to constantly compare ourselves to the world around us, causing us to continuously shift, change, and recreate ourselves to fit in? If that's the case, well then, that's just maddening.

Let's continue using our ice cream and spaghetti example to illustrate this madness.

I'm spaghetti and I'm comparing myself to ice cream. My quick comparison could go many different ways, but it may sound something like this: we're both foods, but ice cream has way more flavor options, and I'm a dinner item that's much more substantial.

At first glance, I recognized our similarities. We are both foods. I saw something positive in ice cream: its variety. After seeing the positive in the ice cream, I justified myself by saying that I'm more substantial. This was at a quick glance.

If I looked a little deeper and thought carefully in order to put a value or worth on our similarities or differences to come to a desired conclusion, like if I were seeking an answer to the question, "Do I measure up as a person?" (or in this case, as a food), I might say that people like ice cream more than spaghetti. *Kids get super excited when they talk about ice cream, but they have to put up with me at dinner to get the ice cream. We're both foods, but I don't taste as good as ice cream. And I have gluten. Everyone thinks that's bad.* And so on and so on.

I would see the deficiencies in myself when I start comparing. *More people like ice cream. More people get excited about ice cream.* There are many options to complement ice cream, like cones, sprinkles, and hot fudge. People gather and meet for ice cream. They stand in long lines just to spend lots of money for ice cream. *Ice cream is better. More people would rather have ice cream. I am not what they want. How could I make myself desirable to them?*

If I, being spaghetti, could control my own narrative, I might say, "I will create a spaghetti bar, where people can pick and choose the sauces they add to me. I'll be in cities nationwide. I will create a buzz around a new way to eat spaghetti, and more people will start liking me."

This reaction would be based on my perception of what I have seen and the experiences I've had.

But what if I lived in Italy, where people travel just to eat spaghetti? My perspective changes. My value changes.

There's always another side to it...always. But if I'm not careful, I try to control the narrative around me in order to justify my perceived value. Stick with me here. My perceived value comes from how others are responding to me, and if I can get them to think positively of me, then my worth is validated, and if I can't, then it's not.

Another way to say it is that my perceived value comes from comparing myself to those around me to get the desired result (approval and validation) within my social sphere of influence and even in my own crazy mind.

It's not always objective, it's often subjective, as the standard always changes depending on outward perceptions and circumstances.

We try to control our own narratives, which have the ability to change daily. Today, thanks to social media, we can change the filter, in more ways than one, before we post. Not only do we have the ability to turn a cloudy day into a sunny one by using our phones, but we have the ability to make ourselves look, sound, and act differently according to what's trending on any particular day.

Although our reach is global now, the unseen algorithms keep us contained in a small pool of people we want to influence or who want to influence us. It's not just social media, it starts with us who use the tool of social media to impress the world around us, longing to fit in even when we say we want to be different. Humans desperately try to create a gauge to effectively measure their worth and value, and comparison can easily become that gauge. It can shift, change, and be manipulated in our hands to create a false sense of security. This sense of security whispers, "You're okay because you're like them, and if you're not, just add it to your selfie self and keep trying."

It's just like the spaghetti trying to be as desirable as the ice cream in a world that seemingly doesn't appreciate it. Little does it know how valuable it is outside of its contained point of view, so it struggles and tries to be like ice cream, creating options and flavors and adding to what was already significant, substantial, and satisfying on its own.

We all play roles to be accepted—inside and outside of our preferred social media platform. The world in which we live is built on acceptance. It's built on loving everyone and everything. Anything goes, and it seems to be celebrated. We can post pictures and stories of ourselves and get thumbs-up and heart emojis to prove that we're okay.

But what do you really think deep inside? Deep inside that selfie self? What's the image you've dreamt up over the years; the image of who you think you should be? Is it just me, or do you want to look a certain way too? Do you want to have a certain job? A certain level of respect in your communities? A level of leadership in your circles of influence? Respect from your friends and family? Does the self you see in the mirror look like you want it to? Is there someone else or something else you're trying to be?

After careful thought, possibly over a long period of time, have the similarities or differences of *you* compared to the *ideal you* created a deficiency in the *real you*?

Is that deficiency your responsibility to correct, to manage, or to justify?

No, it isn't, but we all have a tendency to believe it is. We can actually long for it to be because, if it is, we have control. If comparison is the tool we use to gauge our self-worth, then we have the perceived power to become anyone we want to be, and becoming *that person* is worth the effort.

What are you striving to become like, either in appearance or in action, that you can't seem to achieve? Why is it important to you?

The perceived power to control who we are is the lure. The attractiveness in "her" draws you in, lulling you to sleep as you consider, ponder, and carefully think about the differences between the *you* you are today and the *ideal you* that you believe you can someday be.

Selfie Self + People's Approval = Perceived Value

Let's return to the biblical sisters for a moment. We'll review these infamous sisters and see how they relate to what we're talking about.

As I mentioned earlier, Jacob loved Rachel. Oh, he really did love her. He worked seven years to marry her. Seven years went by quickly as he kept his sights on her. It was time. The celebration started. The wedding feast. The reception. The wedding night.

So exciting. So romantic. So wonderful.

But the Bible says, "In the evening he (Laban) took his daughter Leah and brought her to Jacob, and he went in to her. . . . And in the morning, behold, it was Leah! And Jacob said to Laban, 'What is this you have done to me? Did I not serve with you for Rachel? Why then have you deceived me?'" (Genesis 29:23, 25).

Imagine Jacob's face when he saw that he had woken up next to Leah instead of Rachel. The customs were different back then, and I am assuming there was a lot of wine involved, and that's how Jacob was tricked. Let's focus on the fact that Jacob was stunned to see Leah's weak eyes lovingly staring into his the next morning.

What must Leah have been thinking? Women didn't have much say in those days, so she had to do what her father told her. She could have assumed her father was trying to pawn her off on Jacob because she would never find a suitor of her own. Laban even says that it was the custom that the older daughter would marry before the younger one (Genesis 29:26). We can conclude that no one had come for her yet. Did her father see this as the best chance to marry Leah off? Maybe.

Imagine the heartbreak of having to trick the person who is so obviously and openly in love with your beautiful sister. It would've been fitting if Leah had played a Disney-like fairytale in her mind the night her father made her trick the man who loved her sister.

She could have imagined that her big bad father was making her trick the handsome prince. Even though Jacob had always overlooked her, he'd soon realize that it was always Leah whom he loved once he woke up and saw her. Sound familiar? How many teenage movies have been made about the ugly duckling turning into a swan? *She's All That*, *Never Been Kissed*, *Miss Congeniality*, *A Cinderella Story*, and all its spin-offs. I could go on and on. Those are from the twenty-first century. What about *Cyrano de Bergerac* from the nineteenth century writing about someone in the seventeenth century?

A Tale as Old as Time… "I'm Not Good Enough"

For years, humans have seen the deficiency within ourselves when compared to others, and in some creative and culturally relevant way we insert ourselves into the narrative of "her" by way of deceit. Yet the outcome in Hollywood is always good—a predictable happy ending that proves we were perfect all along and "they" just needed to get to know us, and "they" would fall in love. We have watched these stories for years. They change slightly from year to year, and we can't get enough of them. They feed the fantasy of "her" in all of us. For two brief hours we're transported into a world that shows us what it would be like if the object of our affection could see us as we really are and still love us (even if we have to trick them into it).

How many times did you watch those movies when you were young and insert your crush and situation into the storyline, and then hope started rising right there in your own living room?

But the Bible is true life. And Jacob didn't see the beauty within Leah, and his heart wasn't changed when he caught a glimpse of that small but noticeably deep twinkle in her weak eyes. NO! He freaked out and jumped out of bed. He probably didn't even talk to her and just left her lying there naked as he stormed off to talk with her father. To make matters worse, Rachel could have been standing quietly, confidently, and beautifully by, antagonizing Leah without a word as they both watched this man fight for the love of his life, Rachel.

Leah had no words, just a deep hurt. The deep pain confirmed that she wasn't enough—not for her father, not for Jacob, and not in herself. She was alone. Alone in her pain. Alone in the reality of not living up to what people wanted from her or what she expected from herself. She had closely and over time been comparing herself to Rachel. And it was confirmed that morning: she was not "her," and she never would be.

Happy Endings Don't Always Exist

Have you ever had a moment like this? A moment that didn't have a Hollywood ending. A moment that broke your heart so deeply, so effectively, that you knew. You knew what you feared all along but had hoped others would prove wrong. The moment it was confirmed that you were, in fact, not enough.

Take a moment and ask the Holy Spirit to reveal a time when someone or something reinforced your belief that you are not enough.

I'll share a couple of my moments with you. I have a few.

My mom and dad were divorced; he was an alcoholic. Long story short, my mom, my brother, and I moved to another state. My father never visited or asked about me. Never. My nine-year-old self knew deep inside, and without words, self-reflection, introspection, or journaling, that I wasn't enough for him to love or to fight for me.

I was never student of the month. I know, right?! I can hardly believe it myself. I would sit in class every month, dreaming, fantasizing, and preparing my surprised reaction for when they called my name, but they never did. I was so sure that I had met all of the qualifications, but I was never chosen. I wasn't thought of. I didn't have the wow factor on top of the prerequisites for third grade student of the month. I just wasn't enough.

Oh...this is a good one. I liked a boy. Well, I've liked several boys throughout my life. I was cool and they were cool with me. I was their friend. As I liked them, they told me about the girls they liked. I kept quiet. I would think of my Hollywood mentors and believe and hope that someday they would see what was right in front of them. They never did. I wasn't pretty enough? I wasn't thin enough? I'm not sure what it was. I suppose that *I* just wasn't enough.

I have so many more examples and stories that perpetuated the belief that I wasn't enough. They proved the I-don't-measure-up theory I had about myself. If only I did. *Someday. When I become like "her," I will be enough.*

Enough about me. Let's get back to this biblical love triangle.

The story gets stickier. Jacob complains to Laban, and Laban feebly explains why he deceived him. Jacob says he still wants Rachel. Laban agrees that he can have Rachel in one week, but he'll have to work another seven years for her. So that means Jacob is bound to work for Laban another seven years and to be the husband to both Leah and Rachel.

Jacob loves Rachel so much that he is willing to do it.

Leah is still unwanted, but Jacob is stuck with her in order to marry Rachel. Leah knows this and so does Rachel.

Rachel is the pretty one. She's the favored one. She has the upper hand, and I can assume she feels pretty confident in sharing this man with her ugly sister. Again, it wasn't super abnormal for a man to have more than one wife in that time, although that is never what God intended for His people. Anyway, this is the situation they find themselves in now.

The Bible says that "When the LORD saw that Leah was hated, he opened her womb, but Rachel was barren" (Genesis 29:31).

Oh snap! Game changer.

What's the next most important thing for a woman in that time period besides getting married? Having kids, specifically having *boys*. Leah gave Jacob a son—six of them. Rachel was barren. Rachel was now useless in her purpose. Rachel now, metaphorically speaking, was the sister with the weak eyes. "When Rachel saw that she bore Jacob no children, she envied her sister" (Genesis 30:1a).

Rachel's foundation was shaken, and her deficiency was unearthed. Rachel's "her" became fertile Leah. Leah's fertility was now a threat to Rachel as Rachel compared herself with Leah. Beauty was no longer the conclusion or the standard they were using, but the ability to give Jacob children.

As the sisters carefully consider their similarities and differences to come to the conclusion of who is the better wife to Jacob, they find a similarity in that they were both played by their dad to become this man's wife, and their differences are outward beauty and fertility. One sister is fertile and the other isn't. Look at that…fertility is trending, and that's without social media. The target has shifted, and Leah is succeeding while Rachel now feels inferior.

It didn't take much to shake Rachel up. Infertility was something that she never even knew to be true of herself. Her confident, poised, and "beautiful in form and appearance" self couldn't have kids. She saw a deficiency in herself. She didn't internalize it though. She blamed Jacob. She said to Jacob, "Give me children, or I shall die!" (Genesis 30:1b). What a reality-show-worthy statement! I'm sure there was a table flip in that scene too!

So, both Leah and Rachel have a deficiency in themselves that's brought to the surface by looking at each other. Funny enough, each was the other's "her." The same people with different circumstances changed their minds and changed their roles. The sisters looked at each other long enough to see what they lacked for the given circumstance and felt like they weren't enough.

Not enough for who? For Jacob or for themselves? Does it matter? They don't feel like they are enough. They don't measure up.

But measure up to what? In this case, they didn't measure up to each other. The significance they would feel from being the one Jacob loved or the one who could bear him children was out of their reach. Rachel was loved by Jacob, and Leah could give him heirs. The thing each of them could do didn't satisfy them. If only they could do what the other one did, then they would measure up and have value and significance. Their hope was in the becoming, and they hadn't become yet.

Uh-oh, that sounds familiar. Value is a moving target. They put more significance on becoming what they weren't rather than on being themselves. It's subjective comparison—a moving target that tells you if you're good enough or not.

Sounds dangerous.

We have the privilege of looking at their story objectively. It seems laughable through the lens of the twenty-first century.

I Say, "I'm Enough," but Am I?

As I look at my "her," I can say I'm definitely more self-aware than Leah and Rachel were. I have grown. I have matured. I have evolved into a confident woman. I have listened to podcasts and read self-help books. I am overcoming my tendency to compare myself to "her" with bold and outspoken self-love—with another selfie reel.

In this reel, I climb a mountain like the ones in Nature Valley commercials. I stand at the top. Feet spread apart and hands held high, I scream, "I am enough! I am me!" I walk to a soundtrack of beats that says, "I make moves, and I am uniquely me. Unapologetically me. And if you don't like me, there is something wrong with you." I have snapped out of my tendency to compare myself with others. I speak in mantras, and I refuse to listen to the inner critic. I am aware of my inner critic, however, and I also understand what imposter syndrome is. I look those things in the face and say, "I am enough."

Do you believe me?

Aren't I still comparing myself to a moving target? Society tells me I can declare that I'm enough. YouTube and its hosts of self-admitted experts tell me I'm enough. The society in which I live, in which we live, says we're enough in ourselves, just as we are. The society in which Rachel and Leah lived said it was okay to marry your cousin and produce lots of male babies while you sat at home waiting for your husband to come home from your sister's house. Is it society that sets the standard? Does my evolved and current selfie self that says, "I'm enough," have the ability to back up this truth? Isn't it still subjective?

Way down deep inside, I don't really trust society's point of view. Deep inside, I still feel kind of wrong screaming, "I'm enough," when I know I'm not. Because to what standard am I comparing this statement to? If I think carefully to put a value or worth on the similarities or differences to come to a desired conclusion that I am enough, what am I comparing myself to? Myself? I am enough in myself? How? In what way? Just

> Ask yourself, do I believe I'm enough just because I say I am?

28

because? So, there is no standard? Is the standard my feelings? My feelings change moment by moment. Is the standard the simple fact that I'm a human being? So what? There are lots of human beings. Some are murderers. Some are rapists. Do I not compare myself to them and think I am better and they are worse? Do I take a cue from the world I live in and stop trying to change myself and instead try to control society's approval of the "just as I am" me?

No.

I always compare myself to my "her." My her has been nurtured. My her has been seen with my mind's eye. Created by me my whole life, she has grown with me, developed, and matured with me. Despite the new "I am enough" me, the me that proclaims the inner critic to be a liar, she still reminds me at any given time that I am not enough. As situations and circumstances change, she reminds me I am still, and will always be, deficient in myself.

I don't measure up to the standard I set for myself, even if I try to proclaim that I do. Even when I see my life on the screen projected by my mind and it approves of me, there is still something missing. Something is still quietly screaming; my gut knows it to be true. I can say it a million times, but I am not enough until I see "her" on that screen. I must see her living life in front of my eyes, the way I always dreamed it to be.

Like Leah wasn't enough for Jacob, even though she was able to give him children, she was still not the object of his affection.

Like Rachel. Even though she was beautiful and Jacob wanted her, she was barren and could not produce for him what was needed.

When is enough, enough?

Chapter Two

CRITICISM

Enough comparing. Enough using faulty measures. Let's talk more about the belief system that tells me I'm not enough. It forces me to look around the world I live in to try to create a life that proves that I am good enough. It's the same belief system that created a "her" to try to live up to.

As we have learned, if I compare myself to others, it's out of fear and focuses on what I'm lacking. Qualities, traits, and characteristics stack up to create an ideal me and keep "her" alive. Even when I say I'm enough, I know I'm not because the me that I know and believe I am can't stand up to the weightiness of that statement. Deep down inside, I believe I'm not enough.

This belief system has made tracks in my mind. It has embedded a pathway in my brain so that whatever I do to look like "her" doesn't work because I believe it won't.

I believe what I've been told. I believe I'm not good enough to be student of the month or sought after by my father or desired by the numerous love interests in my past.

What we believe is so powerful. Each of these moments reinforced a knowing that something about me was wrong or incomplete, and a belief system was created.

This belief system was then reinforced by what others thought about me and said about me. I had a panel of judges who shaped and molded the beliefs I had about myself. You know, those people whose opinions of you carry weight no matter what you tell yourself or how much you harden your heart toward them. Their opinion counts. It counts enough to mold your actions in response to them like an Olympic judge.

To compete in the Olympics, super-athletes work hard to hone their skills. They're at peak perfection when they arrive at the games, and then it's time to perform in front of judges, experts, and the world. What the viewers would likely say was a perfect performance, a judge would find fault with, and it's their opinion that counts. These athletes are being judged to determine if they are better at a particular game than another person from another country. They know what they're getting into. They long for it, train for it, and are ready for it.

I don't think I realized my life was an Olympic sport to be judged by the nonexperts all around me—people who see in part, not the whole. These people who compare what they see to what they think they should be seeing. In one short moment, at a glance, or even in a small excerpt of my life, they unleash their opinions on me; opinions I never even asked for. And for some strange reason, I listen. I listen just as intently and expectedly as an athlete does once they walk off the field or the mat, wondering how they scored.

I listened and I believed. *If only I could be like they said I should be, then I'd be worthy of their approval.* I believed the inner knowing that I was lacking something, and if only I could be filled with the thing that was missing, I'd be great. Then, I would deserve the crown, the gold, and the title!

That's how the belief system was formed, but what was the result of it?

Criticism. It flowed in me and through me.

Who sits on your panel of judges? What were some of their criticisms toward you?

I secretly criticized myself internally for not being what they thought I should be, but I outwardly criticized them for judging me. *How dare they? Please keep your opinions to yourself.* These people weren't strangers or those I met in passing. The "they" I'm referring to were family, close friends, and people who had great influence in my life. *How could they say these things? Aren't they supposed to love me just as I am?*

The pain was too great, and I numbed it any way I could. But mostly with criticism.

Let's define "criticism." It's "the expression of disapproval of someone or something based on perceived faults or mistakes."[iii]

The expression of disapproval usually comes out in our words but stems from our heart. Simply put, I can look down on myself and speak out against myself and agree with my panel of judges. I can do the same to others as well. I can be pretty judgmental too.

I love the end of the definition: "on perceived faults or mistakes." So, I am expressing disapproval of someone or something based on something that *isn't necessarily true*—just perceptions. Sounds like those Olympic judges again. Am I one too? Am I a judge of someone else's life? The thing I thought was so unfair of them to do, am I doing it too?

I do it to myself, and I do it to others.

I love to perceive a fault or mistake in someone else. That way, I can express my disapproval of it.

My heart is full of criticism toward the person I'm not, because of who I think I should be. Have you ever heard the phrase, "You can't give what you don't have"? If I don't have compassion toward myself, then I can't give it to others. What I *do* have though is a hefty amount of criticism, so that's what I dish out to those around me.

As I look around, there's a whole world of "not enough" people to criticize. I can criticize the person at the store for taking too long to check me out. I can have an issue with a friend who didn't do something the way I would've. I can tell them how to live. I can tell them how to act. I can shape their life.

I can be brutal. The worse I feel about myself in any given moment, the more critical I am of others.

It could be about someone's physical appearance. *How did she get someone like him? Why is she so fat? With all that money, why doesn't she fix her nose?* Or it could be about their intellect or professional abilities. *How did she get that position at work? She's not that smart.*

If you're nicer than me, maybe it sounds more like this. *She's so pretty, I wish she would wear less makeup, so as not to cover up her natural beauty.*

Just because you say she's pretty, who are you to say she wears too much makeup? Even though it sounds complimentary, you are still criticizing her.

Aren't you still trying to control a perceived fault in something or someone? Aren't you still expressing disapproval in a perceived fault?

Or how about this one. *I've worked hard for this position. I know she has too, but I'm the better fit. Why did they give it to her?*

If you are both qualified for the job, what makes you think you're a better fit in the eyes of the person making the decision? That's not an opinion—it's criticism.

Why is your way better? You are comparing yourself and your opinion of what is good and true to someone else. It is a perceived fault or mistake.

Criticism has become my favorite pastime. Is it as bad as it sounds? Aren't I just expressing my opinion? I've learned to do it the nice way. I've learned to pretend that I'm being nice—I am a Christian after all. I've learned to tell myself that I am discerning, that I am wise and insightful, and that I can see people's flaws easily. I feign humility as I label it a God-given gift.

Don't They Know I'm the Victim?

This outward critical expression of those around me sustains the life of the victim I'm trying to save by becoming "her." This criticism breathes the very breath into "her," which satisfies my need for value and perpetuates my need for acceptance. I'm not conscious of this fact because it's the fruit of my faulty belief system, so I keep criticizing those I say I love in order to be the me I always knew I could be, and honestly, who I need to be.

Look around. As a society, we criticize the people in the world around us because they don't think like us.

In an effort to be all-inclusive, we have excluded anyone who doesn't think like us. We have villainized them. We easily take offense at their opinions of us. We let offense and unforgiveness fuel national movements and celebrate the victim that triumphs and bullies all of us to

Who are you most critical of?

35

think as they do. And if someone refuses, cancel them. Erase them.

All because of perception—good and bad.

In an effort to make the world a better place, we have lost our own identity in trying to become who we think we're supposed to be. And if anyone tells us otherwise, they're wrong. We have the right to become anyone we want to be. How is that bad? Why is wanting to be "her" so bad?

We have already discovered that the things we seek and desire can change suddenly. Trends come and go. The people and circumstances we use to compare ourselves to can change.

And change is usually not a bad thing.

But when we try to create an ideal version of ourself by using comparison to gauge our own ideas and thoughts, this is when the thing that satisfies the need today changes tomorrow. It's like when we create movements and change laws to force others to accept who we want to be today without considering what that might look like tomorrow.

It's not just inward criticism, internal eye rolls, or gossip with friends. It's laws, rights, and history we're creating in our own misconceptions.

Regardless, it's fuel for perpetuating false motives and false lives. It's a distraction to keep us outside of who we were truly meant to be.

Our attempts to be "her," our efforts, our struggles, our lives...all spent creating a life we've dreamed up. This belief system results in criticism of ourselves and the world around us. I have lived this life. I've lived the life of trying to be someone I think I should be rather than who I am. I've felt the discontentment with myself and have internalized the disappointment of those close to me. I've tried hard to become the person I think I should be, and I have failed.

This has led me to failed diet after failed diet, to gastric bypass surgery, and back to more bad diets. It has led me to the wrong friends and careers, to drug use and overdose, to self-help town and to deception, and it has led me to blame others for why I'm not where I believe I should be. As a Christian, it has led me to believe I can pray for change in order to create the life I want to glorify

How have you attempted to become the person you think you should be? How have you succeeded? How have you failed?

God. But truthfully, I have prayed to create the life I've envisioned as acceptable to glorify myself. It has led me to criticize not only myself and others, but the biggest perceived fault I find is with God. And I love Him. So, how could that be? But it's true.

Do I Really Believe God Is Perfect and Good?

Before I read about Rachel and Leah, I read that God created the world. Do I really believe it? In Genesis, the same book where I find these two sisters, I first heard about what life was always supposed to look like. "So God created man in his own image, in the image of God he created him; male and female he created them. . . . And God saw everything that he had made, and behold, it was very good" (Genesis 1: 27, 31).

It was *very* good.

I don't see it as good, and how I've lived my life up to this point might sound something like this to Him.

God, I wish You had made me so much different. I wish You made me like "her." Since You didn't, I will spend my lifetime trying to be

37

like her. I'll spend the life You created, planned, and died for to perfect the creation You said is very good and to make myself even better in my own estimation. In my opinion, God, a life spent trying to be something I'm not will be my expression of disapproval of You based on those perceived faults or mistakes.

Before I knew You, maybe that was okay. But now that I do know You, how could I say this? How could I live like this? But I do. I wish You had made me a little differently. I wish You made me able to do all the things I want to do. I wish You made me in a way that when people see me, they approve of me. I wish You made me someone I can approve of. I wish You made me like her, but You didn't. You made me like You. And for that, I disapprove. I'm discontented, so I pray; pray for what I want. And when You give it to me, I am still frustrated because it doesn't last. Soon enough, I want more. More of what? More of the things that will make me like her.

I say I want more of You. And I think I mean it, but my actions prove different. I want more of everything else. I want "the more" to come from You, but the more I want isn't You, it's me. What I truly want is more of the me I dream to be. More of the me I wish I could be.

Stay here a moment. Let it sting. Can you hear yourself in this prayer?

Did Rachel and Leah Have the Same Problems?

Well, they criticized each other and themselves. They prayed for children for their own edification and not to glorify God. They saw who they weren't and what they couldn't do, so they manipulated the world around them to approve of them—the them they wanted to be. One was loved by Jacob, and the other was able to produce children. They disqualified themselves as they compared themselves to each other. They criticized themselves for what they perceived to be lacking in themselves and criticized each other to alleviate the pain that deficit caused. They also controlled and manipulated their surroundings to create, or to try to create, the life of "her." *Surely that would change it all.*

They pulled Jacob into their crazy. Their servants were caught up in it too. And their children inherited it as well. Here's one example:

Reuben, Leah's firstborn, brought her some mandrakes in the days of the wheat harvest (Genesis 30:14). Such a thoughtful boy.

Rachel was watching, but she wasn't rooting for Leah. She said to Leah, "Please give me some of your son's mandrakes" (Genesis 30:14).

Leah still has some issues with Rachel. Her reply says it all.

"But she said to her, 'Is it a small matter that you have taken away my husband? Would you take away my son's mandrakes also?'" (Genesis 30:15).

I would say there was still some resentment there. She was not going to share. She wasn't going to give Rachel any mandrakes, any time, or any attention. She put her hand in her face, so to speak, flipped her hair, and walked away.

But then Rachel enticed her by saying, "Then he may lie with you tonight in exchange for your son's mandrakes" (Genesis 30:15).

Hold up, not a bad deal. It could be worth giving the mandrakes to Rachel if she'll get Jacob for the night. Leah doesn't even think twice.

"When Jacob came from the field in the evening, Leah went out to meet him and said, 'You must come in to me, for I have hired you with my son's mandrakes.' So he lay with her that night" (Genesis 30:16).

If you're having trouble following the drama, I'll break it down into simple terms: Rachel just pimped Jacob out! For some mandrakes! And he didn't protest. Not one bit. It seems like the world was being run by these two crazy women. Or at least Jacob's world. And for what, mandrakes? What the heck is a mandrake anyway, and is it really worth selling Jacob out for some?

A mandrake is a root found in their neck of the woods. They were thought to promote fertility. An aphrodisiac, sometimes called love apples. Ohhhhhh, I see. Rachel decided to get some help with increasing her chance of pregnancy by using dietary supplements. I suppose it was worth giving up a night with Jacob.

They were like us—or should I say we are like them? At the very core of the issue, nothing has changed. We manipulate our circumstances and the people in our lives to be or do what we desire. We are so focused on what we don't have and on what others do have that we miss out on what makes us the same. It's a web of deception that not only hurts ourselves but those around us, and most of the time, those we are closest to.

I have a "her" because she is the person who proves to the outside world that I am legitimate, which proves to me that I am worthy of acceptance. I don't necessarily realize this is happening though, so I stay on a cycle to perpetuate this illusion. And while I do, I criticize the world around me for not understanding me—the me I have created, the me I have made up, the me that's *her*.

As I continue on this cycle and criticize myself for not being the "her" I dream of being, I look around and see what I'm not and criticize others to make myself feel better. But the worst thing I do is criticize God for not coming through in the way I'd like Him to or, even worse, for not making me the way I want to be.

Let's see how Rachel reacted when God finally gave her what she was praying for.

"Then God remembered Rachel, and God listened to her and opened her womb. She conceived and bore a son and said, 'God has taken away my reproach.' And she called his name Joseph, saying, 'May the LORD add to me another son!'" (Genesis 30:22–24).

She had gotten exactly what she wanted, what she had waited so long for, what she prayed for, and the moment after her prayer was answered, she prayed for more. Was it not enough? I guess not.

Criticism is the fruit of a faulty belief system that stems from a lie. The lie tells me I'm not enough and I have the power to change myself apart from God. It's a life distracted by what I'm not and by what others are. It gives me the liberty to critique God's plan and His ways. But He has revealed to me what I really sound like. I'm not just discerning and self-aware, I'm also prideful and arrogant. Sadly, He's right, so what can I do? How can I take this gift of revelation and not ask for more the way Rachel did? Not more of what I think I need, but more of what I really need—that is, more truth to set me free from the lie. The solution is simple: I asked Him with a heart that truly sought His answer. I encourage you to do the same. Just ask Him. Ask Him with honesty and transparency. He is faithful to answer.

God knows everything about you. Ask Him to reveal the lies you've believed about yourself and to expose the truth of who He is.

Chapter Three

COMPASSION

A lot of things happened after Rachel bore a son. Jacob wanted to move away from his father-in-law, Laban, so he prepared his family to leave. Laban tried to deceive him again. However, Jacob was given a plan from God. Leah and Rachel actually agreed on something. They had the option to stay with their father, but he had sold them and taken their money, so they chose to go with Jacob. Rachel stole an idol from her father's house and denied it. Jacob decided to confront his past and meet with his twin brother again—the one he stole the blessing from. Dinah, Leah and Jacob's only daughter mentioned in the Bible, was raped. Jacob's sons get revenge and put the rest of the family in danger. Rachel got pregnant again. Yes, you heard me right. In all of this family drama, Rachel gets pregnant again.

While they were traveling, she gave birth. She had a difficult delivery, and she didn't make it. She died right after delivering her last son. She named him Ben-oni, which either means "son of my sorrow" or "son of my strength."[iv] But Jacob called him Benjamin, which means "the son of my right hand."[v] They buried Rachel in Bethlehem.

The meaning of Ben's name, given by Rachel, was translated from Hebrew. It has two very different possible translations, and this makes me wonder. God made sure this book was not altered. It is true—even the translations from Hebrew to English. But there's a discrepancy here from the Hebrew word "Oni": it could mean either sorrow or strength. Why would God leave this up to interpretation? Is it because He wanted to give us a choice? A choice of how we see things? Either Rachel said "son of my sorrows," like she regretted longing and asking for a son who would lead to her demise, or "son of my strength," like the son who would prove her strength, vigor, and perseverance after she was gone.

Do We Have a Choice?

Can we take the longing, the wanting, the desire to be "her" and make it our sorrow *or* our strength?

How so?

Can I look at my desire to be someone other than who God created and let it define my life in either sorrow or strength?

Can I go from believing that God created me and saw that it was very good, to criticizing Him for His creation, and then go back to embracing His creation? His creation of me just as I am? Not as my "her" but as His?

I believe I can. I believe that if I take that route, I choose strength.

If I believe that I can't and stay in this cycle, after identifying it for what it really is, I choose sorrow.

What does God say? God said that while I was still a sinner, Christ died for me (Romans 5:8). What does this *really* mean, and why should I care when it comes to "her"?

What does the Romans
5:8 verse mean to you?
Really think about it.

It means He had compassion for me. He didn't just give me what I wanted. He gave me what I needed, even when I didn't care.

God had compassion for Leah and Rachel. He gave them what they wanted, and they misused and mistreated those gifts. They never received from those gifts what they truly needed, which was perfect love from a perfect Father, from a perfect God. They lacked a perspective to see themselves as perfectly loved children from a perfect God in heaven. It was offered to them, and they had a choice too. But they chose sorrow. They chose strife. They never got what they truly wanted. Or at least the Bible doesn't tell us they did.

They were God's chosen people. They were bound by covenant from a God who can't lie or break a promise. They were His. And yet they still chose sorrow. So can we.

Through the Eyes of Perfect Love

Let's go back to the issue at hand—the reason for "her"—for validation and acceptance. She is the mind's creation for fixing, or trying to fix, the "truth" of not being enough in ourselves. We've learned that we are born knowing something isn't right. It's been reinforced by our own panel of judges whom we've agreed with, and then we set off on a track of becoming someone we were never meant to be.

I know that saying "I'm enough" doesn't actually make me enough.

What really makes me enough is the fact that while I was still a sinner, Christ died for me (Romans 5:8). His sacrifice proves I *am* enough.

My Christian life is built on this one verse. I totally get it! But do I really? Do you?

Listen.

While I was still a sinner, while I wasn't enough, while I was separated from God, while my good works and best behavior were like filthy rags in the eyes of God (Isaiah 64:6), He still chose me. I could never measure up to the true source and only source of perfection, which is God. I continued to do it on my own and failed, all while spiritually spitting in God's face. While I was that…Christ died for me.

What did He die for? For me to know Him, to be with Him. Why did He have to die? Because He loved me enough to want me to be restored back to Him. He didn't want to stay separated from me, the creation that He said was *very good*. Even when I wasn't acting very good and turned away from Him and didn't obey Him. I told Him I wanted to do it on my own. I wanted to do it my own way. I even wanted to tell Him that I'm enough in myself without Him. *I don't need You. I can do it myself.* And yet, He still loves me. He still died a very real death, because the Bible says that the wages of sin are death (Romans 6:23). Someone must die. And He became my sin—my "No, thank you, God, I'll do it myself." Sin isn't just the murder, the rape, the lying, the "bad" stuff, but also the turning away from God and deciding not to listen to Him and to do it your own way.

There were other people in the book of Genesis like this before Rachel and Leah. Remember Adam and Eve? They didn't listen to God. They listened to someone else. They made a choice. They paid the price. They died. They died a spiritual death, and we inherited it.

Yet, while we were still sinners, Christ died for us. He had to. He did what we couldn't do. He did it willingly, and He did it with joy. "For the joy set before him endured the cross" (Hebrews 12:2 NASB).

Eve's "Her"

Let's talk about Adam and Eve a little more to see if Eve had a "her" too. Hmmm, I wonder. What happened to those two in the garden? What would make Eve and Adam (can't forget Adam) eat that fruit?

Adam and Eve lived in the garden. They lived with God. They were given everything. They had it all except for one thing, one tree. God told Adam not to eat of it. Then, the serpent came. The serpent who was "more crafty than any other beast of the field that the LORD God had made" (Genesis 3:1) started talking to Eve one day. I'm not sure how. Was it casual? Was it common for animals to speak? It didn't seem to bother or scare Eve that a snake was talking to her, but nevertheless, he did, and we'll take God's word for what it is—truth. But he asked a question: "Did God actually say, 'You shall not eat of any tree in the garden'?" (Genesis 3:1).

He asked a question that caused Eve to question what God had said.

Eve replied, "We may eat of the fruit of the trees in the garden, but God said, 'You shall not eat of the fruit of the tree that is in the midst of the garden, neither shall you touch it, lest you die'" (Genesis 3:2–3).

She replied with what God had said and what she believed to be true because God said it. Simple. Easy.

But in verses 4 and 5, the serpent responds back to her: "But the serpent said to the woman, 'You will not surely die. For God knows that when you eat of it your eyes will be opened, and you will be like God, knowing good and evil.'"

The serpent lied because that's what he does. He told her that she *wouldn't* die. And that she would be like God, which placed doubt in her mind.

Eve's thought process may have gone something like this. *Does God want to withhold something from me? Does He not want me to know good and evil? Does He not want me to be like Him? Why would He not want me to have everything? Why am I not enough the way God made me and with what He gave me? I must need more, and I must rely on myself to get it.*

Verses 6 and 7 go on to say, "So when the woman saw that the tree was good for food, and that it was a delight to the eyes, and that the tree was to be desired to make one wise, she took of its fruit and ate, and she also gave some to her husband who was with her, and he ate. Then the eyes of both were opened, and they knew that they were naked. And they sewed fig leaves together and made themselves loincloths."

The serpent placed doubt in Eve's mind. She likely felt that she wasn't enough as she was. She needed more. She started to believe that she wasn't perfectly made by God, or in the image of God, and by eating the fruit she would be like God, knowing good and evil.

She looked at the fruit and saw that it was good—not something to refrain from simply because God said so. She saw that it was good for food. Hold up…there were trees all around her that were good for food. That tree was never an option for good food. She didn't see it as good for food before the liar came to deceive. So, what was her perception of it before she saw it as being good for food?

She saw it as a tree set apart by God. She was instructed by Him not to eat of its fruit and not even to touch it, and that was okay with her before. Eve had lived happily in the garden, enjoying herself, her husband, God, and the provision He gave them. She had enjoyed the plentiful fruit all around her. She saw the tree that the serpent pointed out long before he did. She knew it was there, but it was not appealing to her—it was just a tree. She hadn't even seen the fruit as something available to her. It was simply a tree. She didn't question what God said. She believed Him. She loved Him. Content with herself and what had been given to her, the tree didn't taunt her, didn't lure her in or entice her with its exceptionally good-looking fruit. It didn't stand out. It didn't scream, "I have the best fruit, and you can't have any!"

But one day, the liar asked her a question—a question that made her doubt what God had said and see the fruit on that tree differently. It was good for food. And she made the decision that it was good for her. And her husband too. Good for food and it could make one wise? She wanted it. She saw something she hadn't before: an opportunity to be like God. She went after it, and she thought she achieved it. Was Eve's "her" God? To be like Him in her own merits, beyond the amazing fact that she was made in His image?

She wanted what He had—all of it. Saying, "No, thank you" to Him, she turned her back on Him and took care of business for herself and her husband. Then, she suddenly realized she was naked. Shame took hold of her, so she took hold of some fig leaves, trying to cover up the fact that she isn't enough. Only now it's true. She and her husband were separated from God because of their sin. Not because they murdered someone, not because one of them had an affair, not because they ate some fruit, but separation came because they listened to someone else other than God. They did what they wanted to do instead of what God had told them to do. It's that simple. And yes, they did surely die—twice! A physical and a spiritual death occurred that you and I also inherited. Thanks a lot, guys! (I likely would have done the same, so I'll hold back the blame.)

Take time to journal your thoughts. What has the serpent been saying to you? Has he made something seem appealing, saying you can be "her" in your own merits?

God was not surprised, and His plan (which was made *before* the foundation of the world) was put into action. Jesus was coming. And then He came. And while we were still sinners, He died for us.

But Leah and Rachel, Eve's great-great-great-great...granddaughters, did the same thing as Eve.

And so did I. And so did you.

God wasn't surprised by us either.

Our Spirit of Independence

So, I guess we don't have a comparison problem—we have a sin problem. Our "her" equates to sin. It's our "No, thank you, God. I'll do it my own way. I will create myself in the image of my own dreams and desires." The question the serpent asks is, "Did God really say you were worth dying for?" Our innate desire is to be like God in our own merits and to create ourselves the way we want to be. It's all the same. We think to ourselves, *I'm not enough on my own. God didn't do it right. I must have it all, and I must do it for myself. I'm not someone worth dying for because Jesus needn't have died if I can change myself.*

Think about it.

Remember when I mentioned that *knowing* something isn't right? The initial feeling of *I'm not enough*? Yeah, well, it turns out that feeling is good! Wait, what?

Yes, that feeling or *knowing* is given to us by God. It's written on our hearts. The Bible says in Romans 2:14 (MSG), "They (gentiles) show that God's law is not something alien, imposed on us from without, but woven into the very fabric of our creation. There is something deep within them that echoes God's yes and no, right and wrong."

We know something is not right. Then, the liar comes and talks to us too. He speaks through those pesky panel of judges. The ones who tell us what's wrong with us—the entire list. We agree with them, and there begins our faulty belief system. Because what's wrong with us isn't that we don't look a certain way or aren't chosen for student of the month. It's much deeper. What's wrong with us is that we're sinners and separated from God. But then the liar says something else. He says *we* can fix it! He says we could fix the problem, become better, receive approval from the other sinners, and voila, we've done it—we've fixed it and made it right. This system of works based on a lie says we can become good enough on our own merits. Works is the real fruit that comes from the knowledge of good and evil. It makes us believe we can reach God-like perfection without Him. That's not becoming like God, knowing good and evil only affirms that we can't do anything apart from Him.

The realization that we can do nothing apart from God was first revealed at our salvation. We recognized we were a sinner and acknowledged Jesus as the propitiation for our sins. And we chose Jesus. However, the choice to try and do it apart from Him continues to be offered to us. As Christians, will we choose grace or works? Will we choose to do it ourselves or with God? Will we choose sorrow or strength?

Let's break down what it looks like to try and fix it ourselves—to be in a cycle of works that produces discontentment stemming from a faulty belief system.

We'll look at how this cycle meets me in my selfie self.

Let's say I am my enlightened, mature self. I look at myself and think, *You got this, girl. So what if your flabby legs jiggle in your lululemon outfit as you walk down your average neighborhood street! So what if your protein smoothie is more like a peanut butter and chocolate high-octane milkshake! You know, the one you spent $8 for on your way to the grocery store to buy more pretend health food. What? It says "organic" on the package! Does it really matter that you aren't the owner of your own successful business but rather a housewife with a side hustle on Facebook Marketplace? I am enough, and that's okay. I am happy. I am content. I continue about my day.*

I tell myself lies. I say that I'm okay being me, and I like doing what I do. I like my mundane life. I post on Instagram about just how amazing it is. I share with an audience, *my* audience, because I'm a star. I'm a beloved child of God, and I have told myself I'm okay.

I say that I'm making great strides in my life. I am happy. I am walking my path. Living my truth. Finding my voice.

I think this me is who I'm supposed to be. The me I am now. Content me. The me that's okay with being me. Until it's not okay. The "her" is me—the me that pretends not to care, the me that pretends life is good.

This is the me that's cluelessly fighting the "her" who innately became me. She's the standard I've set for myself, not God. This ideal version of me is not the real me, but this false standard is reinforced by today's celebration of ME—whoever I decide to be. And I decided I want to be "her." I have woven her into my DNA. As much as I tell myself it's okay that my thighs jiggle a little, I still walk around my neighborhood with the hopes that they'll stop. As much as I want to believe I've arrived and I'm not fighting with her anymore, I haven't. I still act accordingly, constantly comparing my "me" actions to my "her" beliefs. When they don't quite align, I try again. And again. And one more time, I try again.

Where is there discontentment in your life? Does it stem from an expectation of yourself you can't seem to meet?

But while I was a sinner, Christ died for me. I don't seem to remember that though—not when it comes to "her."

Let's see if my homegirl Leah did the same thing when God saw she was hated and opened her womb.

Leah had a son and named him Reuben, for she said, "Because the LORD has looked upon my affliction; for now my husband will love me" (Genesis 29:32).

She is validated in society because she can bear children for Jacob. She had a son—oh, what a wonderful day! She's walking in purpose. Performing. Doing something that looks good in the eyes of her husband and to the world around her, but mostly it satisfies herself. It satisfies the longing to be accepted and to produce something for herself that in turn will elicit a response from others, which will prove she's okay. But will it?

God saw her affliction, and He gave her a son. In her mind, Reuben will be the reason Jacob will love her. What? God Himself saw how Leah was hated and opened her womb. He gave her a son—not a daughter—and Leah is so grateful for the gift because, in her mind, the gift will get her what she ultimately wants: Jacob's affection.

I do want to point out that because of this gift, she is now fully functioning in her role as wife. She's checking all the boxes and getting the approval of those around her for being a good wife. Unfortunately, validation in that form is not what she's seeking. She's still seeking the affection of her husband. Is it safe to say that she still wants to be loved like Rachel? Will Reuben do the trick? Will it be enough?

Leah had a second son and named him Simeon "because the LORD has heard that I am hated, he has given me this son also" (Genesis 29:33).

I guess Reuben wasn't enough. So, did Simeon seal the deal?

She had a third son and named him Levi, and then she said, "Now this time my husband will be attached to me, because I have borne him three sons" (Genesis 29:34)

Seems like Leah created a cycle for herself. If I do *this*, then *that* will happen. And if I try again, *this* will happen. Wait, one more time—if I do it just one more time, I will get the desired result. She tried. Tried again. And then, yes, she tried once more.

Leah wasn't enough in herself. But if she got the thing she thought she was lacking, *then* would she be enough?

What would prove that Leah was enough? Simple: a sense of belonging, which would come from feeling like she was wanted; wanted by her husband and wanted by her family. She probably didn't feel like she belonged in her family because her father didn't seem to want her when he pawned her off on Jacob. Or maybe her father was always comparing her to her sister, Rachel. Who knows what that early narrative was, but it's clear that she was not wanted and didn't belong anywhere.

Do you think she knew that she was described as having weak eyes? Gasp. Did she realize she was being labeled? Did she know she was described in a negative light, at least her physical appearance was, and that it's in the Bible, one of the oldest books in the world?

Do you think her story would have been different if she had felt accepted and wanted? If she was approved of just as she was? If she was single? If she never got married? Or if she had married someone else? If her weak eyes were accepted and celebrated? Do you think that would've made a difference to her and caused her to stopped trying?

Her expectations and desires were certain. She wanted to be accepted. She wanted approval and to disprove the lie she believed, the one that told her she was not enough. But she likely set those expectations and desires on the one thing she could never get: the affection of her husband. Even God—yes, the God who can do *all* things—couldn't fill those expectations and desires with the gift He gave her. Wow! She's trapped in this cycle.

Leah wanted to belong. Leah wanted to be wanted. She strived and longed for the life she imagined. She did what she thought would finally do it. Do what? Allow her to become "her." Spoiler alert: it never happened.

She never stopped trying. I haven't either.

I ask myself these questions sometimes: *What cycle am I on? What have I tried, and what were the results?* Maybe you're asking yourself these too.

The cycle goes like this.

FACT: I'm not enough on my own.

FALSE BELIEF: It must be because I'm not like "this," and in order to be enough I must achieve "this."

NEXT FACT: Achieving "this" doesn't make me enough either.

FALSE BELIEF: It's because I'm not "her." What else does she have that I'm lacking?

Back to the top and the cycle continues.

If I am like "her," if my selfie self were to be realized, I would be enough in my own right and in my own estimation. I have never quite achieved it though. I'm still trying. Let's dig a little deeper into my crazy—the image I created and the cycle that keeps me chasing its mirage.

If you remember where we started in this story, "she" was all the things I wanted to be. She was all the things that produced the result I thought I wanted. But what was it really? What result did I truly want?

I want to believe that God loves me just as I am, but I want to look and act like "her" and gain acceptance from others because of it.

Although my her has evolved over the years, becoming a combination of many different people, there were a combination of set qualities she always had. These qualities would result in a me that would be enough and could be approved of.

Let's break it down by her qualities and my perception of how people react to said qualities.

She was pretty. Boys like pretty. People like pretty.

She was trendy and well-kept. Attractive. People approve of attractive.

She was thin. Thin looks like self-control. People take you more seriously when you're thin.

She was a go-getter and goal oriented. Bold. People make room, and they stop and listen to bold.

She was disinterested and didn't seem to care what you thought. Confident. People believe in confidence. They want to be around it, and they support the efforts of assertive goals.

But people *liked* me. I can honestly say I don't remember too many people who didn't like me. But I don't think *I* liked me. My "her" showed me a me that I could like; a me people would have a legitimate reason to like.

Approval. Well, hmmm. That's another story. A simple statement spoken by close family and friends, and even some strangers, was misconstrued in my mind. It told me that I wasn't accepted. *You'd be so pretty if you were thin.* That eight-word sentence confirmed that I wasn't enough. But I still had a chance. I wasn't counted completely out in the eyes of the person speaking—if I only lost some weight, I'd be back in the game.

So, I did. I lost weight. Enough weight to be accepted—but I still wasn't. I wasn't bikini-to-ball-gown thin. I was the kind of thin that only someone who used to be fat would understand. There are scars and skin, lots of loose skin, that come from that kind of transformation. And that's not the kind of thin that I'd imagined, so it didn't count for me. It did seem to count for my critics though. Maybe because they couldn't see the layers of Spanx I wore to hide the effects of massive weight loss. So, they finally approved of my outward appearance, but they didn't like my job or my career path. I suppose losing weight was my Reuben. My firstborn. My first attempt for acceptance, for validation, for approval.

My selfie self was a go-getter. She was goal oriented. Bold. People make room for, and they stop and listen to, bold.

So, I went to college. I graduated with a bachelor's degree in three years. I was on the fast track to corporate success. Even still, no one seemed to care. I walked into corporate America feeling overwhelmed and underprepared and scared out of my mind. I didn't get the response I was hoping for from my panel of judges.

Again, I listened intently to those judges, not God. Silence. I continued on and looked for a job. Overwhelmed and without a clue of what I wanted to do, I started a nonprofit. I listened. I listened with expectancy. I scored a 4.8. Sub-par. I quickly reevaluated my decision and went to work with the family—the thing I knew, my comfort zone. I listened. Silence. I tried again. I decided to travel, and I enjoyed not working. I listened again and scored a 9.8. What? I was a laughable antidote. I only take two vacations a year. One for the first six months of the year, and the second for the last six months. LOL. It was a score that suited my judges' definition of success, but not mine. I guess my career was my Simeon. I was better at not working, and my life was becoming an amusing story at cocktail parties.

Failed attempt number two. Apparently, I was not a go-getter. I succeeded more when I failed and didn't follow through. The go-getter in my selfie self was not expecting my judges to approve of something so irresponsible. Goes to show that when your definition of success is based on being the person you think you should be and how you think others will react, failure seems to follow.

My selfie self was also disinterested. She didn't care what you thought. Confident. People believe in confidence. People want to be around it. They support the efforts of assertive goals.

58

The third time around, I didn't care what people thought. I didn't care that I couldn't please the critics around me. I stopped listening, or so I thought. But I did care. I really wanted their approval. So, I went on to do my own thing. To numb the pain of knowing that I'll never be her. I no longer cared about her. I left. I ran; I ran so they would stop judging me. *I am disinterested in everything, and I am out. Peace.*

The third attempt was my Levi. I received no validation. No applause. No sustaining acceptance. Silence.

I left them, but they didn't leave me. The need for their approval was still there, even when I told myself it wasn't. I tried to put physical distance between us, but they were closer than I thought. They were in my mind, always telling me what I wasn't.

I tried. And I tried. And yes, I tried again.

I couldn't do it. I couldn't reach the pinnacle of her. I felt like a failure. Why couldn't I be her even when I did the things that she did? *Why don't the people around me validate my efforts? Why do I need them to?* Why didn't I validate my own? Why did I keep trying?

If I didn't know Jesus loved me, being stuck in this cycle would make a lot more sense. My "her" has evolved over time. She started out as one thing, but now she has become me, or should I say the person I'm trying to be. After several successful and not so successful attempts, my her is the image I have cast in my mind as the one who people will approve of. Although I say that I know God approves of me, I continue with trying and failing, unaware that I will never succeed—even though I believe I can. What? That doesn't make sense. Well, kind of, it does. If I didn't believe I could become her, why would I keep trying? So, I have to believe that it's possible. At the same time, I have to remain unaware of one thing: the fact that I'm even trying! If I knew that I was actually trying to become someone

I'm not, then I would stop. So, I need to keep this a secret from myself. I have to cover it up with pop culture crap—self-awareness and self-help. I can't actually know what I'm really trying to do. I just need to keep myself unaware enough in my self-awareness to continue this pursuit unaffected.

The Fourth Son

Let's see how Leah's doing. She had a fourth son and named him Judah. She said, "This time I will praise the LORD" (Genesis 29:35).

And then she stopped bearing.

Here's a quick recap. Three sons in and she still hasn't received love from Jacob. God seems to love her though. And when the fourth son comes, she stops and praises the Lord.

Do you think she always wanted to be like Rachel? Do you think she tried to gain approval from her dad as she did from her husband? Do you think it's possible that comparison can easily turn into competition? Yet another cycle that keeps you bound in your attempt to become someone you were never meant to be in the first place...

But for this one brief moment, we see that Leah stops trying to receive love from Jacob, and she praises the Lord.

Remember, God saw that she was hated. She saw that God loved her by giving her something. The first three times she thought He was just giving her sons to get Jacob to love her. Maybe the fourth time she realized it was enough that God loved her. I don't know. Maybe she paused for just a moment and stepped out of her cycle to say, "Praise God. This child will be called Judah" (Genesis 29:35).

It wasn't too long after that quick praise break that the competition kicked into high gear as these two sisters continued to compare themselves to each other.

Rachel sees that she has borne Jacob no children. She gets mad at Jacob, and Jacob gets angry in return. Genesis 30:2 says, "Jacob's anger was kindled against Rachel, and he said, 'Am I in the place of God, who has withheld from you the fruit of the womb?'" And in a *very logical response* to that statement, Rachel gives Jacob her servant to have a child with. Her servant conceived and then conceives again. So, if you're keeping score, it's Leah four, Rachel two (by way of surrogate). *Ding, ding, ding!* Round Two. Leah sees that she has stopped bearing, so she takes a cue from her sister (no surprise there) and gives her servant to Jacob too. And Leah's servant has two children. The count is now Leah six and Rachel two—total of eight for Jacob.

Rachel won't let it go. I suppose neither will Leah. Rachel is loved by Jacob—what more does she want? Leah has the bragging rights and has borne Jacob sons. They both have merit according to society. They both have "accomplished" something to prove themselves legitimate. Why do they keep it up? Sibling rivalry? I don't think so. It goes to show that it's a deficiency in themselves, and the lie is proving what they've always believed. *They are not enough because of Leah's weak eyes and Rachel's inability to have children.*

The cycle continues. For Leah. For Rachel. For me. And for you.

I am still on a cycle—one that I don't even know I'm on. No wonder why I'm always tired. Why the IBS kicks into high gear even when I eliminate gluten. Why I get things done but still feel like I could've done so much more. Why reading the Bible, going to church, and even serving in the community subtly emphasizes the fact that I feel disjointed.

Are you on a cycle too? You may be starting to identify it. It's a cycle you try to control, but the things you hold onto the tightest seem to slip through those pretty little fingers of yours. You know those things you do that don't seem to work and when you don't get the result you're seeking? You keep trying, and you've even gone up for prayer after your church service thinking you've surrendered that "thing" to God. Do you think it's part of the cycle you are now aware you're on?

Take time to journal through your cycle.

How do we break the cycle? Or to say it in a way that acknowledges God, how do we get breakthrough? Can we do it apart from Him? John 15:5 says, "Apart from me (God) you can do nothing." Uh-oh.

This cycle continues. I can't get out of my own way or out of my own head. I can't line up my me actions to my "her" beliefs in this new reality; the reality of knowing I'm not able to shake her from my mind. I can't pray her away, fast her away, ignore her, or forsake her. So, how do I get rid of her?

So Why Do I Feel Numb?

Staring at my computer screen, I'm typing and asking, "Can it be that awful?" This life I've lived for years, the striving and undermining my own efforts to become someone I was never meant to be, it can't just be a waste. It wasn't simply a cute little distraction or a simple shoulder shrug like when most girls see what they want in others. We always want what we don't have, right? We do, but no. This is so much deeper. For me to say, *even though I know You, God, and Your compassion and love for me, I have been deceived. I've have been fighting a war within myself—one that could never have been won on my own—all the while singing songs that say Yours is the victory.* And in this place in my life, the blind spot was so big that I could've never seen it for myself. Oh, but thank God for His mercy that reveals truth; truth that sets me free. There's freedom in the fact that I can face this truth, even though I don't want to believe it. And you can too.

I don't know about you, but I don't want to believe it. I want to think I'm being dramatic. I want to think I'm overreacting and that most people at one time or another have wanted to be someone else, and it's fine because *haha isn't it funny.* We can make light of it. It's not that serious. We make comments all the time, seemingly innocent ones, that reveal the desire of wanting what others have.

And then I stop and think, *why? Why am I trying to minimize this realization?* Is the serpent asking me, "Did God really say that comparing yourself to 'her' is like saying 'no, thank you' to God, and 'I'll do it myself and become a god in my own eyes'? And did God really say that you need a Savior?"

In the Light of That Truth, What Do You Choose?

Can this truth bring me to such a sorrow that it makes my heart break for what I've been doing, saying, flirting with, and daydreaming about in the eyes of God? That my innocent "her" motivations are truly a "No, thank you, God, I'll do it myself"? That a life built on *maybe, someday, when I'm her* was a life built to bring me to a place of god in myself and not *to* God Himself, even if I know God and believe that while I was a sinner, Christ died for me. With this realization, sorrow brings me to repentance, and in repentance, God's forgiveness comes. The truth that I'm not and will never be enough apart from Him can bring me strength.

Ah-ha! We have to repent. Freedom from "her" only comes through purehearted repentance—not just Jesus' love and acceptance of us. Is repentance simply an "I'm sorry, I won't do it again"? Kind of, but there's more!

We have to name it. What? We must name our sin. It can't be a cute antidote at a cocktail party—the "short, sweet, laughable, self-deprecating yet laced with humor" kind of confession. We must name our sin correctly. We can't just say I'm comparing myself with others and want to be "her," fueled by my weak eyes and validated by my husband's blatant disinterest in me. My sin is trying to be like God on my own merits. I am saying the life, the body, the way that I am is not good enough, and I will change it myself. Taking matters into my own hands, I go on diets, feed myself with the words of self-help gurus, or even the Word of God—or should I say the misapplied Word of God—to strive and make myself in the image of me. Perfect me...who is really her.

Okay, wow. And if I don't properly name it, it will stay and the cycle continues, but if I see it for what it is, I can repent and turn away, killing the cycle and leaving room for God. Leaving room for God to do what? Can I trust Him to do it the way I want Him to?

The cycle continues when I demand life to be the way I want—either by making it happen myself or praying for it to change. Even in my sweet, holy-sounding prayers, I am still telling God what I want, how I want it, and when I want it. Maybe you have done this too?

Sometimes it seems like we pray in circles, trying to get out of the cycle, trying to move beyond this place of "stuck" in our lives. Never achieving validation from the panel of judges or from ourselves (or from either). For me, I believe I've been relentlessly seeking God, but have I? I've really been on a one-track mission to become like "her."

Can you relate? Have your prayers been to get you out of situations you don't think are fair or to become better at something somebody else is good at?

If we don't properly name it, we will continue the cycle until we see it for what it is: sin. Repent. Turn away from it and turn back toward God instead of looking at and pleading with "her." Let's just call it sin now and actually be in our right minds. Stop the insanity, the quest for the impossible, and turn around. We can actually sense the nudging, the quiet and gentle knock on the door coming from behind to help stop us from engaging in the lie—to pause, listen, realize, see the crazy in which we have been participating. The sin. The ugly. The pride. The jealousy. The comparison. The me-in-the-place-of-God moment. We can acknowledge its futility and its disgusting taste and consequences. And to confess all of it. To say NO, I don't want this. I'm sorry I have done this. Done this to me? No. To You, Jesus. Because we sin against God alone, not ourselves or our own expectations of ourselves. But solely to God. That means He gets the "I'm sorry." He is the one we direct our confessions to. And as we come to, emerge out of the fog, the lie, and snap out of the soothing sound of the devil's lullaby, we can confess this our wrong. "I am doing the wrong thing against God. I have sinned in the sight of God. Not my panel of judges or myself, but I have sinned against God and Him alone."

Am I being too harsh? No. Sadly, I'm not. What do you think?

Ask the Holy Spirit to reveal ways you have sinned against God in your cycle.

That's the whole point. As I look back on what I've been calling comparison—or what I lovingly call *The Rachel Effect*—I've seen how the displeasure with myself, my weak eyes, has caused me to listen to the serpent and look around the world in which I live to create a better me. It's the me I feel I should've been in the first place. *I should've started out that way, having it all* (in my own estimation of "all"). I would do anything to get it—even continue in my deceit by trying to pray myself into a life that I've created rather than what God created.

And that's not too harsh. That's God's mercy and compassion.

It's His sweet, patient, kind voice that says, "This is what you have really been doing. Stop that. Turn away from that. See it for what it truly is. And remember that I love you, created you, and made you in *My* image to be who I have called you to be. I died for you while you were still a sinner and invited you into My family to be in relationship with Me. I want to show you who I am, who I've made you to be, and want to do My will here on this earth through you. Perfectly imperfect you: the one I made, the one I love, the one I died for, the one I offer forgiveness to with no condemnation in Christ Jesus."

So, now I'm not bound by that sin or the lie anymore. God is gracious when we confess our sin, and He is faithful and just to forgive us and cleanse us from all unrighteousness. How simple, easy. It is finished. But now what do we do?

Are you like me, living in the shadows of "her" for a long time? For a really long time even though I know who I am in Christ. I am loved. I am forgiven. I am His child. I am a new creation. I've learned this from Bible study, church attendance, and connection to other believers in Christ. God has been doing a work in me.

Apparently, I've been fighting with Him tooth and nail because the new creation I've sang about and have been praying about has been in the image of "her."

I have cried. I have prayed. I have desired and told God that He promised to give me the desires of my heart. And those desires were about "her," so now what? Who am I if I'm not the sister with the weak eyes who wants the love of my husband? Or the barren sister who is beautiful in form and appearance? Or the fat girl trying to be thin and successful, poised and confident?

If I'm made in the image of God, if I'm His creation, then I can only assume He knows me best. He is the one to go to—to ask, to let Him show me, heal me, make me, and reveal to me…me!

Chapter Four

COMPLIANCE

The Death of "Her"

Before we can start to comply, let's first define it. (I love definitions.) To comply is "to conform, submit, or adapt."[vi]

To comply, we must conform, submit, or adapt. I have been doing that according to my own estimations, and conforming, submitting, and adapting to my own thoughts, dreams, and visions, not God's.

What are God's thoughts, dreams, and visions about me? About you? Well, I know God says, "For my thoughts are not your thoughts, neither are your ways my ways. For as the heavens are higher than the earth, so are my ways higher than your ways and my thoughts than your thoughts" (Isaiah 55:8–9).

And Isaiah 55:6–7 says, "Seek the LORD while he may be found; call upon him while he is near; let the wicked forsake his way, and the unrighteous man his thoughts; let him return to the LORD, that he may have compassion on him, and to our God, for he will abundantly pardon."

It is clear that God has compassion for us, as He reveals to us our sin and offers us forgiveness without hesitation. He has shown me that the "me" I was trying to be was not the "me" He created me to be. I have seen it through His eyes. I was trying to be the Creator, but I have forsaken my wicked way and have returned to Him—into His loving and kind arms. I have received His compassion and forgiveness. He has abundantly pardoned me. Thank you, Jesus.

In order to envision the real life God has created and not the ideal life we are trying to create, we need to agree with God and who He has called and created us to be.

But He says His thoughts are not our thoughts, so how can we do this? Let's see what He says in Isaiah 55:10–11:

> "For as the rain and the snow come down from heaven and do not return there but water the earth, making it bring forth and sprout, giving seed to the sower and bread to the eater, so shall my word be that goes out from my mouth; it shall not return to me empty, but it shall accomplish that which I purpose, and shall succeed in the thing for which I sent it."

So, He is saying that the word He speaks directly from His mouth will do what He sent it out to do and it will succeed, and if I remember correctly, He spoke us into being. He spoke creation into being. He breathed His very own breath into man. This would mean we have something to accomplish and that we have a purpose; a purpose wrapped up in each of us that will succeed for what He sent it to do. Not just me, we! *All* of creation. So, what did He send us to do?

What do the verses right after that say? The previous ones say He has compassion and will forgive. Other verses in the Bible tell us that what God says will be done. So, what did He say next? It has to mean something important! Here's what Isaiah 55:12–13 says:

"For you shall go out in joy and be led forth in peace; the mountains and the hills before you shall break forth into singing, and all the trees of the field shall clap their hands. Instead of the thorn shall come up the cypress; instead of the brier shall come up the myrtle; and it shall make a name for the LORD, an everlasting sign that shall not be cut off."

What He has planned is joy and peace! When you have these things, you have contentment and a satisfaction in who He's created you to be and what He has given you. Our inner selves will no longer be harsh, hard, and thorny but strong and beautiful. And that is proof of God working inside us, and He will be glorified in it all, not the other way around.

Really? Is that it? My mind is conditioned to see the external before the internal. I am programmed to believe it only when I can see it. Seeing is believing, right? My wrong expectations of Christian life looks like a world filled with money, men, and miracles. That's my way of asking for provision for everything I want, and how and when I want it, not just what I need.

In what areas is your faith linked to the external rather than in Jesus Himself?

Jesus says in Matthew 6:33, "Seek first the kingdom of God and his righteousness, and all these things will be added to you."

Please, God, Help Me Change My Thoughts

God's thoughts convey joy and peace. My thoughts convey money, men, and miracles. There's definitely a gap here. Help, please!

We will be transformed by the total renewing of our minds. "Do not be conformed to this world, but be transformed by the renewal of your mind, that by testing you may discern what is the will of God, what is good and acceptable and perfect" (Romans 12:2). Transformation happens in our mind, not through our circumstances. Changing our surroundings and ourselves isn't lasting, but changing our minds and aligning them with what God says is what's truly enduring and the only way to eternally impact our circumstances. Sounds like hard work. It's not though. Let's start with looking at what God says about joy.

I remember David praying in Psalm 51:12: "Restore to me the joy of your salvation."

In Isaiah 55:12, God says, "Go out in joy and be led forth in peace."

What does "go out in joy" mean? We will go out of our bondage, our sin—the total encompassing sin that declared we were dead without the acknowledgement of God's salvation—with joy. Although God has saved us, He is still saving us. He reveals areas of weakness and tells us to boast in them so He (God) can be strong. If we embrace our weakness and don't try to strengthen it in our own efforts, God can fill those areas, and that makes us strong in Him! He reveals wrong thoughts and commands us to take them and bring them into obedience to Christ. We are to destroy arguments and lofty opinions against the knowledge of God. He shines His light on deception and tears down strongholds that have kept us bound to a lie. When His Spirit reveals these things, we are brought into awareness. Then, to repentance and His forgiveness, which leads us out in fresh joy.

Salvation brings joy, whether it's from all-encompassing sin, like the first time you truly believed that Jesus is Lord and confessed with your mouth, or from the lies that keep us in faulty belief systems and produce bad fruit. Let's look at why David said "restore to me the joy of your salvation."

David was a man after God's own heart, and even he sinned, going after what he wanted and ignoring God. Long story short, he saw a woman bathing on a roof and, bam, he thought, *I want her*. Only problem was, she was married. David had her sent to him, as he lived in the moment and got what he wanted. She got pregnant. Woops. In order not to be found out, he set her husband to the front of a battle to be killed. It was pretty bad. He didn't acknowledge it for a long time, but in God's loving kindness, He brought a prophet to reveal to David what was hidden. And David repented. God forgave him, and then David prayed that God would restore to him the joy of his salvation.

After a long while of not thinking like God, not walking with God, and being separated from God because of hidden sin, David's joy needed restoring.

My joy needs to be restored, and maybe yours does too.

How can we comply, conform, submit, or adapt to God's thoughts of us? His thoughts that say we're forgiven, that we've sinned, and only against God have we sinned.

I'm still not feeling joy.

I am appalled at what I have done. I've seen it as ugly. God has revealed the true nature of my sin. He showed me in real and tangible ways. Yet the joy—is it blocked by pride? Or mistrust? Or a combo of both?

What is the joy blocker here?

The dreams I have dreamed as "her" were real to me. The realization of how awful they are has been proven, but it doesn't make them feel any less real. And even though I see that I have been playing God, that I've taken the role of Creator, I still really want a life that looks like what I've been imagining. Even though it's always changing, even though it's based on whims and whispers, I still kind of want it. Do I really trust God to give me something even better? Not really. Or at least not yet. How would I know? The idea of forgiveness of sin isn't really leading me out in joy. But rather in trepidation.

So, complying with God's thoughts and dreams is a bit scary because I either don't know or don't believe that His thoughts toward me are good. For a long time I believed with all my heart that being "her" would be good. The dreams and desires I complied with were good because they were going to make me good. I believed that I wasn't good yet. I believed that if I were "her," I would be. If I stop at the fact that God forgave me of sin and I'm still looking inward, then of course my joy will be blocked. I'm forgiven, but I'm still bad. Or at least that's what I believe.

Belief:
To be convinced of
something

A new belief system needs to be created.

Can I believe, really believe and change my mind to comply with the knowledge of who God is and who He says I am, to align my thoughts with His, to know He is good and He said I am good because of Jesus, and to truly believe the Gospel message—the one I say I believe?! You know…it's the one I believe with my heart, but my mind isn't so sure. My "her" actions didn't believe God is good and that He said I am too. The revelation of her in itself didn't do it. Then what or who will do this? The Holy Spirit! Yes, He can take a belief that's void of definition and form and speak to it, giving my mind the ability and power to comprehend. I need to comprehend, in my limited mind, the limitlessness of the goodness of God.

I need to comprehend that the word God sent forth to accomplish His purpose will actually be accomplished. The same word that not only spoke me into existence also reveals who God is. And He made me to know Him! To worship Him in Spirit and truth. To live an ever-changing life with a never-changing God, Father, Savior, Friend, Companion, Guide, Comforter, Protector, Helper, and so on. The *and so on* reveals more of who He is. Remember joy? The joy comes in knowing Him. Or should I say it comes in having the ability to know Him because I'm saved. I'm His child. I'm washed clean. Now I get to know Him because I can see Him, experience Him, and worship Him on that fact alone. I have joy because I'm saved, and because I'm saved, I have been given the Holy Spirit, and because I have the Holy Spirit, I can be led forth in peace.

In peace, we are led forth. We go out in joy and are led forth in peace. We go out from a place of bondage. An enemy of God, we're now a child of God. What God is teaching me now as His child, I can go out in joy as I leave a place of deception. I am led forth in peace. So, I am leaving an old place and moving forward. I am now moving forward in peace. The lie that I believed has been revealed. The Holy Spirit (who does what only He can do!) is leading me out of a lie into truth, in peace.

Why Is Peace So Important?

We don't experience any peace in our turmoil of striving (to become what we think we need to be) by taking on the responsibility to create it ourselves. Peace. Will peace steady the course for us from revelation to reality?

If you're like me, you've had several revelations in your life, even some that didn't stick. I've read my own personal prayer journals where truth was revealed but never applied. And then it was soon forgotten.

Is peace going to keep us calm *in* our leading? We will be led forth in peace. I imagine this feels like when I'm wearing my favorite sweatshirt—covered, surrounded, cozy, warm, comfortable.

In my old efforts, anxiety led me forth in fear. But is anxiety not so much an attack but a motivator? Not only to motivate us back into peace, but also to warn us that we're no longer in peace? This would mean we don't need to get rid of anxiety. We'd simply need to step back into peace.

Peace is always available. Jesus gave it to us. He tells us in John 14:27 that "peace I leave with you; my peace I give to you. Not as the world gives do I give to you. Let not your hearts be troubled, neither let them be afraid."

If we're led forth in peace, then we're led forth by God. But if we're led forth in anxiety, then we're most likely led forth by fear, dread, doubt, or any other gamut of ungodly emotions.

A new cycle can be created; a new cycle led forth in peace to know God and His thoughts, not ours. We can come out in joy and move forward in peace—all to know God, whose thoughts are not our own. We learn and know that His Word will accomplish His purpose. So…joy, peace, Jesus, joy, peace, Jesus, joy, peace, Jesus. I can circle that over and over for all eternity, just like the four living creatures that circle God's throne singing, "Holy, holy, holy, is the Lord God Almighty, who was and is and is to come!" (Revelation 4:8).

When I read about those creatures, I honestly thought, *How boring! I'm so glad I'm not one of those creatures. It must get old.* If you stop and think about it, it wouldn't be boring at all. They are circling God and seeing His holiness. They are seeing every facet of Him. I don't know if they have actually come to the end of it yet. I'm not sure they ever will.

I don't think we ever will either, especially in this lifetime. Joy, peace, Jesus.

And the new cycle will continue as we align not only our hearts but also our minds with His.

Go out in joy (and out of deception). Leave the places where we're being deceived; there are many.

Be led forth in peace; peace that steadies the bumpy road of renewing our mind. Start the process of scrapping the old belief system fueled by lies and step into the new one grounded in truth.

Become more like Jesus. Look more and more like Jesus with every step we take in compliance, or alignment, with who God is and who He calls us to be. With every lie we hold captive and every truth we embrace and believe, we are becoming more like Christ.

In this new cycle, we can learn how to agree with God about who we are by understanding that His thoughts are higher, that *we* are actually spoken out of His mouth to fulfill a purpose in which He sent us out to do. We can agree with Him about who we are by maintaining joy and walking in peace. As His creation, we will see His goodness in our acceptance of who He made us to be—just as we are.

How Can I Become What He Has Called Me to Be?

He's called me—us—to be like Jesus. And in my new cycle of joy-peace-Jesus, I see who He is over and over again. And as I do, I learn more and more. As I fix my eyes upon Jesus, I become like Him. In worship and in time spent with Him, I go from glory to glory. I become like Jesus, just like He wants me to be. We make a

Insert your name here. God made you, He loves you, and He has great plans for you in a life made to live with Him!

Jesus-and-Lauren creation. It's the forgiven and redeemed Lauren combo. I walk as He walks but with my own style, my unique style; the style that He purposed and spoke into existence. He knit me

together in my mother's womb with this style and a special personality. He buried certain hopes and dreams deep down inside of me—to which His Spirit whispers to and my whole body comes alive. Those things the mundane have tried to kill, and yet they live on. They cry out. They've been waiting.

And in His grace and mercy, He has held them back. He wouldn't let my ambition or my need for comparison kill the truest and purest form of me, the me He created. He held back the me I tried to create so I could appropriately compare myself. Is comparison bad? No, not when I compare myself to the One I was meant to compare myself with, Jesus, and I can't do that outside of joy or peace. Therefore, I come out in joy, and I am led forth in peace to see Jesus. To compare myself to Him. To let God do what only He can do: create. He creates the new creature I am and am becoming, to the glory of His name.

So, how do we do this again?

He gave us an imagination. We have looked around ourselves for a long time, comparing ourselves to the wrong people. We each cry out to God and ask, "Please help me to have an accurate view of myself in You. Help me to imagine. Re-imagine. Redeem my imagination, Jesus, to be the me You created. To love myself as much as You do so I can love my neighbor as myself. To not murder them with my thoughts as I covet them and the things I perceive they have— things seemingly withheld from me."

In the old comparison, the cycle results in criticism. In the new comparison, the cycle results in love. As we compare ourselves with Jesus and stay in the joy-peace-Jesus cycle, love abounds. First it comes from Him to us, then to others, and then back to Him. This is the most beautiful cycle in motion. Not manipulated with deception from the liar, but this cycle is nurtured and protected by the Father.

In this, we are comparing ourselves to the person we should be comparing ourselves to. In a healthy cycle, grounded in truth, protected by the Father, the outcome is love.

Holy Spirit, help us to know ourselves like You know us. Help us to see not only who we are but who we are becoming. Speak to the places where we don't have an accurate image of who we are, and then protect us from the temptation to try and create it ourselves through comparing ourselves to others and not You. Put words where there are none so that we may know and believe who we are individually designed to be in the likeness of God.

In Christ, we are loved. Accepted. Forgiven. Redeemed. Powerful. Sadly, I often forget I am made in His image and have the qualities, the DNA, the talents of my Father, and so do you. We are creative. We have imaginations. We are dreamers. We are wise and have access to unlimited wisdom when we ask the Father who gives generously.

The desire to change, to grow, to learn, and to become is good.

We are who He made us to be. He sees us as complete. He knows the end from the beginning. He knows our name, and He knew it before we even did. This may be a silly example, but when I was single, I had one name. Now, I'm married and have a different name that used to be unknown to me—but not to God. So, we may have a skill, talent, dream, desire, passion, or purpose that's already known to God but unknown to us. And guess what? Our good Father is preparing us for it all as we comply, conform, submit, and adapt to God's thoughts of us.

My friends Leah and Rachel couldn't see like we see today, through the cross, and I'm not sure they were willing to comply with how God saw them: those who He saw and remembered as people He loved. They were stuck in their moment, their lifetime, their desires. It doesn't seem like they saw beyond themselves, and little did they know that a girl from a little state in the USA, a totally unknown territory to them, thousands of years later would learn about and love the story of their lives in the true and holy book, the Bible. What's even cooler is that in the midst of their deception, their sin, and their self-absorbed antics, the generational line of a Savior was born through Leah. Yeah, her—my homegirl with the weak eyes. Jesus came from the line of Judah. As for Rachel, her beautiful self wasn't forgotten by God either. She had Joseph who had a dream and a pretty incredible life. He was a Jesus-type figure. He set the stage for God's people. He was an incredibly intricate part of God's story.

As I look back, I understand Leah and Rachel. I understand their hurts, their pains, their lives. Leah's more so than Rachel's, but we've already established how the tables can turn quickly regardless of perceived advantages or God-given personalities. I still relate to them, and I still love them. However, I don't want to end up like them. The Bible tells me that I'm a co-laborer with Christ. I want to work *with* God. I don't want to miss what He wants to do through me—the real me—for His *eternal* purpose. Not for my limited, finite little life, where I think my selfie self is the most important self to impress in a fickle and fleeting world.

I want to live a life where the mountains and hills before me break forth into singing, and all the trees of the field clap their hands (Isaiah 55:12). Not because of the life I create, but because of the life God creates.

God tells us in the Bible that He'll give us the desires of our hearts. And like only He can, He can say one thing but mean two, and then accomplish them both. He gave me new desires: joy and peace, no longer money, men, and miracles. And He is giving me the desire for joy and peace in a tangible way through my circumstances. May He give us the grace to continue to agree with Him, to see the lies and call them out as such, and to embrace His truth joyfully and be led forth in peace. May we be led in His purpose to the place where He directs us by the power of His wonderful Holy Spirit. This is my prayer. May it be done, according to His Word, in the power and authority of Jesus' name. Amen.

Chapter Five

COMMISSION

A s I'm learning what it looks like to compare myself to Jesus, to look like Him in all circumstances, I must remember to be content in all circumstances. If I'm being honest, I oftentimes react poorly to the places I find myself when they look contrary to God's promises for my life.

Have you ever seen someone struggle with mental illness or even addiction? The biggest problem they face is that they don't know they have a problem. When confronted, they plead to be released from the asylum, stating they don't belong there. *There is nothing wrong with me, and I shouldn't be forced to stay in the hospital to be treated for something that isn't an issue in the first place.* What they can't see is that they *do* have a problem; the place where they are is exactly where they need to be. So, they fight with the doctor who knows what is wrong, and they resist treatment.

I find myself doing the same thing: fighting, struggling, praying, declaring, and rebuking. *I don't belong here, Jesus. This doesn't look like it's supposed to look. It's not supposed to take this long. I asked for patience, not to stay stuck in a job I don't like. I prayed for a promotion, and You promised it to me, so why am I stuck in a job that's going nowhere?*

These kinds of prayers aren't helpful. They sound like they're from someone in a mental health institution and not a surrendered child of God whose heart and mind are saying *Your will be done.*

Why Is This Happening to Me?

What's happening is, I don't remember that He sees a problem I'm not aware of. I don't remember that He knows the end from the beginning, and this is exactly where I need to be to become like Him and to have the capacity to hold on to what I prayed for.

How is God seemingly taking you in the opposite direction of what you are praying for?

Even Jesus went through these confusing steps. Although He didn't enter into confusion and struggle with his Father, it would be understandable if He had. He could have felt like He'd entered a spiritual asylum after His baptism. He was declared as God's Son in whom the Father was well pleased and then led into the wilderness to be tempted by Satan for 40 days (Matthew 3:16–4:1). What?! He was declared as God's Son. He is the spotless Lamb who takes away the sins of the world. His mission was declared. Shouldn't belief and success follow?

Nope. God was preparing Him. He was hungry. He was tempted. He successfully left the wilderness and entered into three years filled with a series of miracles that were met with some worship and some criticism. Some people believed and some didn't, even after He told them who He was...even after He proved who He was.

Jesus was always steady. Although at times troubled by what was happening, He never questioned why. He knew what was going to happen, and in His continued connection with His Father, He knew He was there only to do the will of the Father, no matter what it looked like.

Oh yeah, now I remember…God's will, not mine!

Walking with God in Fulfilled Purpose

When I think of the word "commission"—especially as a Christian—I think of the Great Commission. That's what Jesus told His disciples to do when He was gone. Let's see exactly what He said in Matthew 28:19–20: "Go therefore and make disciples of all nations, baptizing them in the name of the Father and of the Son and of the Holy Spirit, teaching them to observe all that I have commanded you."

If I were to break this down, I fear it would fill another book. However, it's pretty specific, yet incredibly daunting if we just take this verse and this verse alone. It's what He said next, in the second part of verse 20, that intrigues me: "And behold, I am with you always, to the end of the age."

That's what Jesus said. He is with us always.

Always.

Yes. Always.

Always—like when I do nothing at all. He's with me when I waste the days away watching Netflix, and He's with me when I'm zealous for His mission. I have been zealous for His mission. I've spent many years doing things *for* Jesus but not too many years doing things *with* Him.

Prior to the revelation of *The Rachel Effect* but years after first accepting Jesus as my Savior, I was excited. Like, soooo excited! I had a dream, a vision, a purpose, and a passion. A God-given one. I said, "Thank you very much. I'll take that, and you watch what I will do with it." Then, I took off running. I dreamt of that vision, and I selfie-selfed my vision into a supposed offering to God.

I prayed, sought, struggled, and went on a mission to do what God had called me to do as the thin, beautiful, smart, successful, obedient-to-God self I thought I was. I was pretty awesome!

Until I realized I wasn't.

I went on a mission for Jesus, but I didn't take Him with me! I prayed, knowing He was always with me. But I got caught in my own comparison cycle. And my "her's" main goal was to arrive at the feet of Jesus saying, "Mission accomplished." My desire to live a Christian life got super tangled up; tangled up in idolatry and pride.

Of course, I didn't realize my "her" was running the show. I thought I was. I thought I was doing what God had called me to do. I was doing it wrong.

I was obedient but misguided. I entered the spiritual insane asylum, fighting and struggling with my circumstances. I prayed them away in order to create a path to lay my fulfilled purpose at Jesus' feet, all the while forgetting His purpose. His purpose is to make me like Him, to bring others to Him by acting like Him, becoming like Him, loving like Him, walking with Him, and responding like Him in grace and mercy.

Have you ever forgotten to take Jesus with you on your way to do something for Him?

As I see His grace and mercy revealing my wrong ways and wrong thoughts, He is making it right. That's what He does! He is "the author and finisher of our faith" as we read in Hebrews 12:2 (NKJV).

Again, I remember He has revealed the truth. He has led me out of deception in joy and is leading me forth in peace so the world around me can be in awe of His work.

I'm still daydreaming though.

I'm still working out and learning new things. I'm still wanting to be different, but this time it's to be more like Him (with a little of "her" lingering).

How do I co-labor with Christ? How can I be commissioned to do what He's called me to do and fulfill my purpose, especially if I can't stop creating my selfie self even as a Christian?

And then God says things like, "Who told you not to imagine the future? Who told you not to want to be different than who you are right now? Don't throw it all away in fear; fear of doing it wrong or fear of growing and developing, changing, and moving forward in the wrong direction. Don't live in extremes. Stay with Me."

But *staying with* can be confusing at times; it doesn't always look or feel good.

Wait a minute. Let's take a quick break and look at our favorite sisters again.

God was speaking. He was moving and was very much a part of their lives. Remember Jacob chose Rachel, but God chose Leah. He chose her, He had compassion for her, and He opened her womb in her very bad situation—her moment of waking up next to Jacob—

surprising him on that infamously deceitful morning when Jacob realized he had married Leah. God was with her through the heartbreak, the tears, and the intense feeling of worthlessness. God was with her in it all. He favored her even when her dad and Jacob used her, devalued her, and tossed her aside. God not only stood by her side, but He promoted her. It was God who valued her and gave her value to the world around her by allowing her to produce. Leah produced not only in her work, but in heirs—children who would grow up and be the great-great-great-great-great...grandfather to Jesus. God was very much in and around this situation.

She would attribute the success to God when she delivered her sons. However, it was always a bit heartbreaking that she thought her sons could be tools used to get Jacob to love her instead of being examples of how God already did. Looking back through God's perspective, we can see an entirely different, beautiful story, as God always had compassion for Leah. He remembered Rachel as well. He gave her Joseph and then Benjamin. He was with them both.

There was compassion. There was love. There was understanding. There was honor, even in a time when women truly were not respected or appreciated. There was provision, and there was a plan.

Through God's Eyes

As I look back on my life through God's perspective, I see the same.

Remember when I wasn't named student of the month? When I wasn't chosen? Although it sounds so small, so incidental, it's not. It's part of the root in the belief system that tells me I'm not good enough, which started this process of comparing and creating myself into someone who was "worthy to be chosen."

As I read what King David asks of God in Psalm 17:8 to keep him as the apple of His eye and for God to hide him in the shadow of His wings, I see how God hid me in that moment. He prevented me from getting what I thought I wanted, what I thought I needed, which was to see myself as valuable by receiving the special title. Because it wasn't true; it wasn't His validation. Now, as I look with God, I see, at that young age, God pouring out His great mercy and protecting me from the lie that I needed everything and everyone else to prop me up to prove my worth and value. The truth is, I really only needed Him.

However, when I refused His mercy in that third-grade classroom, the enemy turned around and whispered lies that I wasn't enough until I had that "thing," that "award," or "accolade." Thankfully, God was patient. Now, 30-plus years later, I see it. I see it for what it really was: the mercy and patience of our Father.

Take a moment to reflect. Where do you see God in some of your most painful moments?

As I look at my current situations and circumstances that bring me the same kind of pain my eight-year-old self experienced, will I take a pause from the pain and quiet myself down enough from pleading with God to make it stop (and not just to make the pain go away like I want Him to)? Will I realize I've entered the spiritual insane asylum again and pause long enough to change my perspective and then my approach?

If I can be still and remember God is with me, I can truly look *with* God and not just *at* Him. I can say, "God, what do You see? What are You doing? How are You hiding me right now? Protecting me? Making me? Molding me into the image of You?"

It's then I remember that I'm not only commissioned to go into all nations, baptizing them in the name of the Father, Son, and Holy Spirit. I'm not only co-missioned as a co-laborer with Christ. First and foremost, I'm a child of God. The Creator created me, made me new, and continues to make me new, and I can't do anything else without God. I can't fulfill my purpose. I can't move in step with Him if I am trying to create myself in "her" and create my circumstances to validate and comfort "her."

Like in those moments when I've run off after He's given me a vision—those moments when I act more like Joseph, Rachel's son, who had a dream and ran with it, and nothing looks like I thought it would, and I'm no longer co-laboring with Christ for the thing He's asked me to accomplish. In this, I impede the process of becoming. I look around, compare, and impose my own thoughts about how one looks with a great God-sized dream.

But this is the whole of it: to be commissioned, to be with God and to fulfill my purpose, allowing Him to continue to create me. I can acknowledge Him in this process, and I can let Him lead me in peace.

In all of this, I have co-labored with Christ in my becoming. It's the hands-on approach of creating me without being the Creator. All the while allowing the Creator to create in me something beautiful. I allow Him to bring me into circumstances and through them—into furnaces, lions' dens, and confrontations with giants. In the unfair and unexpected, I am becoming the me God has always seen, and in my cooperation, He reveals that beautiful creation to me, and the unraveling of who He made me to be is unhindered. I allow Him do the work in me as I walk out the things the Creator has created me to do, things He has spoken over me. And those words will surely accomplish what He set them for. I can be a living, breathing example of who He is as I allow Him to pull out of me who He created me to be—in joy, in peace, with Jesus, who loves me so much. And He will be seen in me by a world of people who are still trying to create themselves.

My prayer is that as I stop trying to create myself, others will see and want to stop creating themselves as well. Let this be your desire also as God continues to reveal who He created you to be.

God, have Your way in me and through me as You created me to be and are continuing to reveal Your creation plan through my life. You said it was finished, and it is. But let the unraveling of me show the replay in slow motion of exactly what You meant by "it is finished." When it comes to me and those around me, may we do what we were created to do: worship You and glorify You always, and with all of who we are. In your name, Jesus. Amen!

Chapter Six

CONNECTION

C onnection is key in maintaining a co-missioned life. As Jesus says in John 15, abide in Me. This type of connection is critical for us when our future looks uncertain on our way to our certain future in eternity. Here is another reference in John's gospel, which illustrates well what a connected life with Jesus in the face of uncertainty looks like.

John's gospel says that while Jesus was at the table with His disciples in what would be the Last Supper, He predicted one of them would betray Him. John, the writer of the gospel, was sitting next to Jesus. Actually, the Bible says he was "reclining" with Him, and he asked Jesus who it was that would betray Him. "To whom I will give this morsel of bread" (John 13:26), He replied. As John looked *with* Jesus, he also looked at the situation through Jesus' perspective. This wasn't an easy topic for John; he didn't fully understand the beauty and the reality of the cross in this moment. Still, he looked *with* Jesus and not just at Him to see where Jesus' focus was.

I want us to look with Jesus as well, do you? As we live this co-missioned life, let us recline with Jesus, staying connected to Him, resting in Him just like He told us to in Matthew 11:28–29, fixing our focus on things that are important to Him, not us.

Let Him steady our steps when we land splat in the middle of turmoil and feel like we've entered a spiritual insane asylum again. This place of rest will give us a quiet trust that will be our strength (Isaiah 30:15) instead of telling God how we don't belong where we find ourselves.

Here are a few things we can do to put joy and peace into action.

1.   Accept the situation. *This is what's happening. This is where I am. This is who I am right now. God, I accept this circumstance and trust You are working it for my good.*

2.   Keep unforgiveness out of your heart; unforgiveness toward God for being in the situation, for the other people, and myself within a particular circumstance.

3.   Feel the pain. There are many emotions in addition to joy and peace. What are they? *God, be with me in all of my emotions. It's okay to not feel okay. I still have joy in this trial, and I have peace guarding my heart and mind as I pray with supplication and thanksgiving.*

4.   Obtain knowledge. Ask yourself these questions: What do I need to learn? How can I grow? What can I learn from being in this circumstance? When have I previously experienced something similar?

5.   Allow God's wisdom to partner with the knowledge to bring revelation.

Acceptance

We have to accept and surrender to where we are in the moment to remember that He is with us. But I tend to have spiritual short-term memory loss, do you? I forget why. I forget that James 1:2 says, "Count it all joy, my brothers, when you meet trials of various kinds, for you know that the testing of your faith produces steadfastness. And let steadfastness have its full effect, that you may be perfect and complete, lacking in nothing."

This is joy and peace in action, not just a gift or a feeling that allows us to float in a trial-free life and become numb. No. This is the gift of God to live life *with* Him and not just for Him.

It's the path in which God leads us to be perfect and lacking in nothing.

What current trial do you find yourself in? How can you rejoice in it in regards to James 1:2?

Accept where you are. It's okay, He knows. This is a tool that can be used in every place for His will to be done. Where the answers to your prayers can be found and the work of becoming more like Him can be done. He really does know the end from the beginning. We don't, so why not let Him do His thing and trust that you're in good hands?

Guard Against Unforgiveness

In the moments of life that seem unfair or unexpected, unforgiveness has a way of creeping in. When these moments last longer than you'd like and involve other people, especially when those moments aren't a direct result of your actions, it's imperative to keep unforgiveness out of your heart.

Matthew 6:14–15 says that if you forgive others for their sins, God will forgive yours, but if you don't forgive others, neither will God forgive you. So, don't let the rotten fruit of criticism grow out of those branches again. Remember, we're not perfect either. We don't want to let the sin of unforgiveness separate us from the very One we want to stay connected to. Oh, it can be hard! The struggle to want to blame others for the rotten place you find yourself in is real. It's normal to want to blame others, but we have the power of the Holy Spirit to help us to not do that! He understands it and will help us!

We can also have unforgiveness creep in toward ourselves and God. When this happens, be clear and open with God about how you're feeling. Romans 8:1 reminds us that there is no condemnation for those in Christ Jesus, and James 1:17 tells us that every good and perfect gift comes from the Father, so we don't have the right to hold onto any perceived fault of our own or of God. We might want to, but the truth that triumphs in this situation doesn't give us that right! Say these scriptures out loud; bury them in your heart. What they say about you and God might not line up with what you're thinking or feeling, but even if it doesn't feel good doesn't mean they're not true.

Feel the Pain

What emotions are you feeling in this difficult circumstance? It's okay to have emotions other than joy and peace, especially during such times. Trust is not blind faith and the absence of feeling—it's believing God is good while you're feeling something contrary to that truth. In a life lived with God, we have the privilege to let Him know how we're feeling. Christian life isn't pretending we don't get scared or don't question or dislike the circumstances we're in, but it's about being honest with ourselves and God.

Take time to think about what emotions you're feeling in this trial. It's important to identify them.

The beautiful part of a relationship is the depth of our honesty and His in the give and take. We can give Jesus our honesty with confidence, and He gives us peace that guards our hearts and minds. In Philippians 4:6 (NKJV), we are told to "be anxious for nothing." Anxiety is one of those feelings that can be produced from mistrust and fear. If we're being honest with ourselves and God about our emotions, we don't need to be anxious about anything, and with prayer, supplication, and thanksgiving we can make our requests known to

God. Then, His peace that surpasses understanding will guard our heart and mind through Christ Jesus (Philippians 4:6–7 NKJV).

Now that's an action plan to being led forth *in* peace.

We don't need to be perfect and have it all together; what a relief! We can freak out. We can feel pain. We can be honest about it and tell Jesus all while doing so, and we can thank Him that He's in control. *Jesus, You understand, and You've got this.* Then comes the peace that surpasses understanding to guard our hearts and minds. We can stand firm in the place God has us, trusting the Victorious One to guard two of our most vulnerable spiritual organs (our hearts and minds) so we can continue on with Him.

Knowledge and God's Wisdom Go Hand in Hand

Knowledge and God's wisdom must be used in tandem. Remember, apart from God we can do nothing. That means applying knowledge to a situation or circumstance without God's guidance and expertise would be foolish.

Let's visit Proverbs chapter 3 to put it in context for us.

In verse 7, we are given a warning: "Do not be wise in your own eyes; fear the LORD and turn away from evil" (NASB).

Beginning in verse 13, we are given a promise:

"Blessed is a person who finds wisdom, and one who obtains understanding. For her profit is better than the profit of silver, and her produce better than gold. She is more precious than jewels, and nothing you desire compares with her. Long life is in her right hand; in her left hand are riches and honor. Her ways are pleasant ways, and all her paths are peace. She is a tree of life to those who take hold of her, and happy are those who hold on to her. The LORD founded the earth by wisdom, he established the heavens by understanding. By his knowledge the ocean depths were burst open, and the clouds drip with dew. My son, see that they do not escape from your sight; comply with sound wisdom and discretion, and they will be life to your soul and adornment to your neck. Then you will walk in your way securely, and your foot will not stumble" (Proverbs 3:13–23 NASB).

Obtain Knowledge

You're in this place for a reason. With God, nothing is wasted. He is sovereign and knows every step you take and every place you find yourself. He has promised to work it all out for good too!

What can we learn while we're here? If we're not fighting with our circumstances or trying to get out of them, then there's something of value we can receive while we're there. If we were admitted to a hospital, we would receive our doctor's diagnosis and treatment plan, and the same can be said for us in the situation we find ourselves in now. Is there healing that needs to take place? Is there simple instruction needed for what might be coming around the corner? Could your current circumstance be preparing you for the next place God is leading you?

Is there a relational situation you are in? What can you learn about that person to help you relate to them? How can you pray for them? Is it your job that you feel stuck in? What can you do to become the best employee there or to be better skilled in your position?

Be aware of your surroundings. What is happening? What can you learn?

What are the facts, information, and skills that can be gained from this situation? What can you learn here that can't be learned in any other way, time, or place?

I don't know about you, but during some of the most unpleasant places I've learned something new. When I was in my thirties, I lived with my nana and took care of her. It was hard, as I didn't know then what I know now. Most of the time I did it kicking and screaming because my independence was taken away and my life seemed to be on hold. I learned some new things like how to be a caregiver and to care about someone else's needs besides my own. I learned that I had some past hurts holding me captive, and I was healed from them in the same room I grew up in. I learned how to be a housewife. My prayers sounded like this, "Jesus, I'm young and untangled; it's time to live life, so why do I still have a curfew?" I learned how to submit and honor someone I love in a real and tangible way. And I prayed to be married, listened to sermons, and went to seminars. All throughout this time it was in dying to my independence to care for someone else that prepared my single and self-sufficient self how to become one with a man.

God's Wisdom

Allowing knowledge to partner with God's wisdom is what brings revelation, which ultimately brings transformation. It's the wisdom of God that brought revelation to what I learned at Nana's.

The wisdom of God helped me to perceive the time I was in. Later, when I married my husband, it was the wisdom of God that put this knowledge into action—the application of what was learned at Nana's years before.

When we give these new skills and understandings to God, by allowing Him to combine His wisdom with our new knowledge, His wisdom will give us understanding and revelation.

Then, not only do we receive wisdom for the circumstance, but we also receive wisdom for the becoming; the becoming like Christ. My knowledge awakened my need for healing and the wisdom to know it was time to let God infiltrate that space in my soul that brought healing. It brought me deeper into the redeemed version of myself that looks more like Jesus.

Do you need wisdom? We can all pray as Paul did in Ephesians 1:17, asking God to give us the Spirit of wisdom and revelation so that we will know Him better.

It's in our going to God and getting to know Him better that we become more like Him. It would be nice and easy to just pray it into existence, but He doesn't work that way. He loves us and is a relational God.

The revelation of who God is and who we are in Him is most often built from testimonies of our experiences with God that can be told to others and also be retold to us. Through these experiences we can move forward and confidently trust in God's character that we now know experientially rather than theoretically.

If any of you lacks wisdom, let Him ask God, who gives generously to all without reproach, and it will be given to him.
James 1:5 NASB

That's the value, the profit greater than silver and gold, more precious than jewels that Proverbs talks about. We then get to experience the ways of pleasantness and the paths of peace when we put these promises into action in all circumstances.

Surrendered Sanctification

We can trust that what He has planned for us is good and purposeful so we can truly surrender to God as He makes us more like

Him. We can trust our good God to do good things even if our circumstances look and feel bad. We can honestly say, "Even when it's bad, it's good," and we walk confidently, knowing we are walking with God. We are not at a deficit in any situation or problem we face because we can pray to God and not at Him. We no longer tell Him that we don't belong there. Instead, we ask Him what He sees through the situation and reveals how we can co-labor with Him in the becoming.

In the hard and the scary times, and in the unfair and the unexpected situations, He is with us. He has equipped us, and He is making us more like Him.

Therefore, we no longer have to compare ourselves and our circumstances to our Christian sisters, even the ones who are beautiful in form and appearance, and we don't have to stop wanting to change either. If anything, God wants us to change because change is good. So, keep daydreaming with God to see where He's taking you and how He is making you!

Make some time this week to daydream with God!

You can still dream. You have an imagination—a God-given imagination to do things with God that even your imagination isn't big enough to contain all that He has for you. Wow!

But in order to do this, you must trust God in a way that allows you to stay connected to Him and walk with Him in confident surrender. Does the thought of giving up control make you nervous? Don't worry. With God, surrender isn't scary, it's a privilege.

Chapter Seven

CONTINUED CONNECTION

The Beginning of the *Real* Me

It's been one year since I stopped typing. One year since I closed my laptop and started living *with* Jesus and left all hopes of "her" behind. One year since I've started to live in the joy-peace-Jesus cycle, fueled by love and acceptance.

I didn't instantly become a Pulitzer Prize author. I didn't miraculously lose weight, nor did I become who I thought I wanted to be when I shut my laptop for the last time and started my hard-core journey of living with Jesus. Instead, something so much better happened. I started seeing things as God saw them. I was able to look at my mundane, ordinary life, along with my jiggly thighs, and see what God sees. Love. Life. Potential. Opportunity. The joy and peace steadied me as the pounds started to pack on and the scale went up. The joy and peace led me through the heartache of closing my business. The joy and peace fixed my hope in Jesus when each month would pass and I didn't see the pink plus sign on my pregnancy test. The joy and peace caused me to look with Jesus and say, "Here I am, and it's okay. Keep unforgiveness out of my heart." What a blessing to sit with Him while I felt the pain of sorrow and loss and ask Him to lead me in finding the appropriate knowledge for the situation I was in. He so freely and graciously gave me wisdom so revelation could come. I sat with Jesus. I sat with Him when the whirlwind, fire, and tornado came until my patience wore so thin and the joy and peace felt like they needed to be refilled. Then and only then, the still small voice came. *Align yourself with Me.*

And like a newborn baby, I entered into this new world of freedom—big and open—no longer confined to the small space of life with "her." Instead, I found myself running in the vastness of the wide-open spaces of life with Him. At first, I felt a little unsteady. Freedom is a big place, light and airy, like a cool, crisp fall day with bright blue skies and big, thick white clouds. When you breathe in, you can feel the cool air refreshing your lungs and bringing clarity to your mind. As I looked around I thought, *I like it here.* I took it all in but did not move until God directed me. *Align yourself with Me.*

I wasn't quite sure what God meant by that, but He started revealing Himself to me. First, He gave me the most amazing gift. I was chosen as client of the month at my gym. Years after the heartbreak of not being chosen as student of the month had resurfaced, God allowed me to be client of the month. Nobody could begin to realize what a gift from God that truly was. I cried and said, "Thank you, Father! How You give us the desires of our hearts." Only this time, it didn't validate me as being someone special in the eyes of the gym staff; instead and more importantly, it was in the eyes of my Father. I was thankful for their words of encouragement and edification; oh, but the joy that came from knowing I was seen by my Father in heaven and that nothing is too small of a desire that He longs to fulfill.

As I rejoiced in the biggest way for the smallest thing, I continued walking with Him. Things continued to look the same in my life. They almost seemed to get worse if I was looking with "her" and not with God. I wasn't getting pregnant, I had closed the business that I felt God gave me as a dream to help and serve people in a way that would give Him glory, and I was gaining weight, even though I was killing it at the gym.

I've struggled with my weight my whole life, and it is one of the biggest reasons I had a "her." *Life would be so much better if I were thin.* I don't say that anymore though. I live in freedom with Jesus; even so, I still want to be thin. There have been years of prayer and revelation attached to the desire to be thin, and with every diet and application of revelation God has given me, still nothing. The ups and downs of the scale continue to be my reality. The frustration and the confession that I will always struggle with my weight still weighed heavy on my heart, until one day I heard something. *You're not fat.* What? Pause. I agree. *I'm not fat.* Alignment.

What just happened?

I'm no longer in alignment with "her." I'm not agreeing with what I've believed to be true. The words spoken over me and the belief system I've created have been broken through my repentance from her, allowing me to see the lies I've been believing. "I'm fat" is a big lie that I've been holding onto for the majority of my life. But Jesus. He had space and my attention in the place I had never surrendered control (even though I said I did many times over), and suddenly I could see that I was grasping this lie so tightly that nothing He has shown me or told me in the past had room to take root. Now that my grip is loosened, I can see that I'm not fat, even though the scale would tell me otherwise. How can I be fat if I'm made in the image of God? He's not fat! He didn't make me fat. Finally, the years of self-sabotage make sense. How could I lose weight if I believed I was fat? I would do everything in my power to be the person I believed myself to be!

Putting the Five Steps in Action

I have accepted where I am. I'm seeing the scale and the current reality, but with God. I have disengaged with the lie, and I've stopped hugging the lie. I've asked for forgiveness from my Father for believing a lie and turning my back on Him in order to do so. I've repented and turned back to Him and have hugged Him instead, and my thoughts are now aligned with His. I've felt the pain of the "not yet" and the regret of time wasted and abuse to my body, with the ups and downs of years of dieting. I have obtained knowledge about how to work out and how to view food in a healthy way. I've learned about my body, and He has led me to doctors who have found infections I never knew existed in my body that have prevented weight loss. Most importantly, I've learned that God is the Redeemer of all things. My mind is being renewed by disengaging with the lie and aligning myself with truth. I am not stuck, and I am learning to believe that I am thin so I am acting like a thin person—no longer feeling guilty eating or labeling food as good or bad. I'm eating with Jesus to the glory of His name for fuel and fellowship. Living *with* God in alignment with His truth.

How was the revelation of wisdom applied to knowledge? I had the realization of the label and identifying statement I have always believed to be true: I'm fat. It has been called out as a lie, and I believe my new revelation. I'm not just saying it because I think I should—I actually believe it. I truly understand and am living the truth that God is the Redeemer. The reasons, the trauma, and the health implications that I've been searching for all these years to figure out why I'm fat and can't lose weight have just been answered. Now that I believe I am thin, it won't be long until what I believe becomes my reality.

In the meantime, as the scale and the world tell me differently, and as my mind fights to focus on what thin me looks like, I don't think it's going to look anything like Gisele the fashion model, and that's okay. I'm imagining with God now, and His thoughts are higher and His ways are better. His joy brought me out of that lie and His peace leads me forth, steadying me in trust that shapes me in the image of Jesus. As I wait to see what shape and form my body will take, my spirit is shaping up to trust like Jesus did. Joy. Peace. Jesus. In the new cycle filled with not-yet, wait, and almost, I am looking more like my Savior and nothing like "her," and I'm having the time of my life!

There are many more stories I'm not able to share and so many more yet to come. This life of freedom lived with Jesus as He created me allows me to pray more clearly, trust more deeply, and love more fully.

As you take this journey, saying goodbye to the person you think you should be and embracing the person God has created you to be, I pray that you allow joy and peace to steady your becoming as you compare yourself with the only One who matters: Jesus. In a life free of comparison, where love can flow freely and you can fully embrace who Jesus is and who He has created you to be.

Acknowledgments

So many people prayed for me and encouraged me while I was writing this book. Many people took their time to read it and give me feedback, which I am so thankful for. However, I would like to thank two people specifically. First, my husband, Eric McNeely. Without him, this book wouldn't have made it to print. His prayer, encouragement, and overall support is the reason you're reading this today. Also, his willingness to eat chicken nuggets for dinner when I was just too tired to cook helped a ton! I would also like to thank my mother for babysitting my son in the height of his terrible twos to ensure this book was edited well and actually saw the light of day. Without these two hugely important people, this book would have only been a personal revelation stored in my heart rather than on these pages. Thank you.

To learn more about author Lauren McNeely, to check on her upcoming projects, to download the 30 Day Devotional; Unraveled, or to request an interview or for other speaking requests, please visit:

www.LaurenMcNeely.com

Author Bio

Lauren McNeely is a soft-spoken extrovert who genuinely enjoys getting to know others and cheering them on in their journey with Jesus. Lauren started writing when she was young but honed her skill of stream of consciousness writing from her ten-plus years of journaling. One of her favorite times with Jesus is with pen in hand and a new journal to pour out her heart and pray for those she loves. She has taught Bible studies with Bible Study Fellowship for over six years, which is where she first fell in love with Rachel and Leah during an eight-month study in the book of Genesis.

When Lauren's not serving in church or writing, she's usually chatting away with old friends or strangers, using her hands to punctuate her thoughts, and laughing through the awkward moments deep conversations can bring. She is also a wife and a mom to an exuberant son, who is following in her talkative footsteps.

End Notes

---

[i] "comparison," Oxford Languages, languages.oup.com, accessed March 21, 2024.

[ii] "consideration," Oxford Languages, languages.oup.com, accessed March 21, 2024.

[iii] "criticism," Oxford Languages, languages.oup.com, accessed March 21, 2024

[iv] "Ben-oni meaning," Abarim Publications, last updated November 22, 2023, https://www.abarim-publications.com/Meaning/BenOni.html.

[v] "Benjamin meaning," Abarim Publications, last updated November 22, 2023, https://www.abarim-publications.com/Meaning/Benjamin.html.

[vi] "comply," *Merriam-Webster.com Dictionary*, Merriam-Webster, April 6, 2024, https://www.merriam-webster.com/dictionary/comply.

Made in the USA
Columbia, SC
10 December 2024

47700128R00069